Endorsements

Understanding Eschatology is an excellent introduction for anyone wanting to understand the scriptural support for a premillennial pre-tribulation rapture position. Dave Reineke matter-of-factly explains the biblical reasoning in a way that covers all the bases while not drowning the reader in theological confusion.

Pastor Trevor Killip
Hope Community Church
West Salem, WI

∞∞∞∞∞∞∞∞∞∞∞∞∞∞∞∞∞∞∞∞∞∞∞∞∞∞∞∞∞∞

In ***Understanding Eschatology***, Professor Reineke presents a highly readable yet deep and exact treatise of future events that are prophesied in both the Old and New Testaments of the Bible. This book skillfully harmonizes the Scriptures pertaining to end of the world and the fulfillment of God's purposes. I found this book to be very informative, God honoring, and I believe it will be a blessing to all who read it.

Maranatha!

Theodor Habel, M.D.
La Crosse, WI

Understanding Eschatology

A BIBLICAL LOOK AT THE END OF THIS WORLD

AND THE BEGINNING

OF THE WORLD TO COME.

DAVE REINEKE

ENGLISH STANDARD VERSION

Understanding Eschatology

A BIBLICAL LOOK AT THE END OF THIS WORLD AND THE BEGINNING OF THE WORLD TO COME

BY DAVE REINEKE

ISBN: 978-1-961110-30-4

LIBRARY OF CONGRESS CATALOGUING-IN-PUBLICATION DATA:
LCCN: PENDING

DISPENSATIONAL PUBLISHING HOUSE
P.O. BOX 3181
TAOS, NM 87571 USA
WWW.DISPENSATIONALPUBLISHING.COM
TOLL-FREE: **(844) 321-4202**

ORDERING INFORMATION: U.S. TRADE BOOKSTORES AND WHOLESALERS, QUANTITY SALES. SPECIAL DISCOUNTS ARE AVAILABLE ON QUANTITY PURCHASES BY CHURCHES, ASSOCIATIONS, AND OTHERS. FOR DETAILS, CONTACT THE PUBLISHER AT THE ADDRESS LISTED ABOVE.

COVER DESIGN: DISPENSATIONAL PUBLISHING HOUSE, INC.
INTERIOR LAYOUT: YE OLDE TYPESETTER, SHOW LOW, AZ

THIRD PRINTING, JANUARY 2025

PRINTED IN THE UNITED STATES OF AMERICA

3 4 5 6 7 8 9 10 11 12 13 14 15 16

Dedicated to my friend and brother in Christ,
Floyd Nolen Jones

The Lord used you to mentor me like no other.

Note: *All Scripture references are from the English Standard Version of the Bible.*

Table of Contents

Acknowledgements

I am deeply grateful to my daughter Anna Dobbs, my friend Theo Habel, and my pastor Trevor Killip for careful review, editing, and comments to improve this manuscript. I also want to thank my beautiful wife Chris for her steadfast support and always being there for me and the children God has given us for the joy and blessing that they bring to our lives. All praise, honor, and glory to our great Savior, Jesus Christ.

Preface

I wrote this book for Christians who are truly seeking to understand God's blueprint for the future. I want to encourage Christians to be like the Bereans and search the Scriptures to see if these things are so. This topic is very broad, and the details are spread throughout the Bible so it can be difficult to see how they fit together. This is my best attempt based on my current understanding of the topic. While I have no seminary experience, I have conducted research over many years as a university professor and those skills can aid in the study of the Scriptures. My understanding of this topic has also benefitted from many excellent Bible teachers. My prayer is that setting my heart to understand (see Dan. 10:12, Ezra 7:10), diligently studying the Bible, and trusting that the Holy Spirit is guiding me that I am led to the correct understanding of the issues I am sharing with you.

Eschatology is an area of the Bible that has always captivated me and driven me to rigorous study. In 2019, I decided to create a ten-part series of lessons for a Life Group from my notebooks containing about 15 years of study notes. From there it was a natural step to keep going and compile that information into the book you are now reading.

Awaiting His return,

Dave Reineke

Introduction

What is *eschatology*? Think of it like any other "-ology". Biology, Geology, Sociology, etc. It is the study of something. In this case it is the study of the *eschaton*, or the last things. Some call it the End Times. The Bible refers to this in a few ways, one of which is "the end of the age" (Mt. 13:39, 49, Mt. 24:3, Mt. 28:20). However, the end of the world doesn't mean that everything will come to an end, be annihilated, and cease to exist. The Bible also speaks of "the age to come" (Mt. 12:32, Mk. 10:30, Lk. 18:30), which will come after this present world ends. The Greek word translated as "age"can also be translated as "world", so some English translations render these as "the end of the world" and "the world to come."

It is not an easy topic to study and there has been much debate among believers as to just exactly how passages of Scripture related to the end of the age should be interpreted. It is not the goal of this work to review all the systems of interpretation or to compare eschatological views, nor is it the goal to simply restate what God has already written in His Word on the subject. The purpose of this book is to show the connections among the various features of the end times and help the reader understand the prophecies God has given.

One difficulty in studying eschatology in the Bible is not a lack of information but rather a large volume of information scattered throughout the Scriptures.

Some things are clear, other things are inferred, and some things are not revealed. Moreover, other aspects of eschatology are like what Peter said of Paul's letters: "There are some things in them that are hard to understand" (2 Pet. 3:16). Nevertheless, if it is something you want to know more about, be like Daniel and set your heart to understand (Dan. 10:12) and the Lord will give you understanding (2 Tim. 2:7).

The events of the end of the world and the world to come are in the category of Bible prophecy since they obviously take place in the future (at least relative to when they were written). Some prophecies about future events are embedded within the flow and context of the events that passage is about and so there is something of a dual nature or a dual fulfillment of them. Prophecies like this refer to *two different* events. For example, consider Hosea 11:1, "When Israel was a child, I loved him, and out of Egypt I called my son." From the time it was written until the time it was declared to be fulfilled in Matthew 2:15, it is doubtful that anyone reading it would have even realized it was a prophecy. Most people reading that verse before Jesus Christ was born of the virgin Mary probably just thought it was only a reference to the fact that God led the Israelites out of Egypt in the Exodus. The gospel writer Matthew, however, explains in Matthew chapter 2 that the flight of Mary, Joseph, and Jesus into Egypt to evade the soldiers sent by King Herod to kill Jesus and subsequent return to the land of Israel after Herod's death was the ultimate fulfillment of the prophecy given in Hosea 11:1. This fulfillment took place hundreds of years after it was written. Though this particular prophecy was about the First Coming of Christ, it is a good example of a dual fulfillment prophecy and the challenges a prophetic text can present.

Eschatology is not only a difficult area of study, but also an area that is often neglected. Since it is not a salvation issue, so some will say, "Why study it?" Think of it this way. God saw fit to reveal many details of the last days in the Bible, so on that basis alone it is important. If it's important to God, it should be important to us. For the Christian, it is a way to know God's heart and plan regarding the end of the age, which brings comfort (1 Thes. 4:18) and hope (Titus 2:13) as well as an understanding of the times we are living in (1 Chron. 12:22) and motivate us to be holy (2 Pet. 3:11-18).

You can gain an understanding of eschatology by reading this book, but you'll never know for sure if it is true until you open the Bible and verify it for yourself with our final and ultimate authority – God's Word (Acts 17:10-11) . Since God has revealed many details of the end of the age, this book is packed with Scripture references. It will take time to study them, but it will be worth it!

Because I am a work in progress, this documentation of my understanding of Scripture is also a work in progress. If you hold another view on any of these topics, hopefully these pages will at least help you understand why these conclusions are reasonable.

The remainder of this introduction will define some common terms that are integral to understanding the eschatological picture and three subsections on God's design for Israel and Gentiles in the New Covenant and what they reveal about the future. In the next chapters, an underlying framework for the End Times will be presented by examining the feasts of the Lord, the places in Scripture where Israel is scattered and gathered, the Seventy Weeks prophecy given to Daniel, and the Olivet Discourse given by Jesus. Following that we will move chronologically through the Tribulation, the Day of the Lord, and the Millennial Kingdom into eternity future. We'll conclude with a study of the Rapture and an assessment of where we find ourselves on God's prophetic calendar.

Common Terms

These terms are commonly used when discussing the End Times. If you are not already familiar with them, the following descriptions will aid your understanding of the rest of this book.

- **Antichrist** – 1 John 2:22. Literally "*The* antichrist*"*, indicated with a definite article here in the Greek text. He is also known as the beast out of the sea empowered by the dragon, which is Satan (Rev. 13:1-7), the little horn (Dan. 7:8, Dan. 7:20, Dan. 8:9), a king of fierce or bold countenance (Dan. 8:23-25), the prince who is to come (Dan. 9:26), man of lawlessness (or man of sin) and the son of perdition (2 Thes. 2:3), wicked one (or lawless one) whose coming is after the working of Satan with all power and signs and lying wonders (2 Thes. 2:8-9). The Bible indicates that there are always antichrists because they are against Christ, but there will be a specific Antichrist in the last days that will rise to global power and be controlled by Satan.

- **Millennial Kingdom** – Rev. 20:4-6. Jesus Christ reigning on earth for a thousand years. Messianic Kingdom is another good name for this. Jesus calls this period "the new world" (or "the regeneration") in Mt 19:28.

- **Rapture** – 1 Thes. 4:17. Believers who are alive and remain will be "caught up" to meet the Lord in the air.

- **Tribulation** – Mt 24:29, Mk. 13:24. A seven-year period of unparalleled trouble on the whole earth, particularly focused on physical descendants of Israel. This time is also referred to as "the time of distress for Jacob" (Jer. 30:7), "time of trouble" (Dan. 12:1), the "fury" (Isa. 26:20), the "indignation" (Dan. 8:19, 11:36), and it is the 70th week of the "seventy weeks" prophecy given to Daniel (Dan. 9:24-27). The second half is called the "Great Tribulation" (Mt. 24:21, Rev. 7:14).

Israel

God has chosen the nation of Israel, the physical descendants of Abraham, Isaac, and Jacob, for three reasons. One, to provide a lineage for Jesus the Messiah (Gen. 3:15, Gen. 12:3, Gen. 28:14, Rom. 9:5, Gal. 3:16). A second reason was to receive, write, protect, and preserve the Scriptures (Rom. 3:1-2, Rom.

9:4, Acts 7:38). Thirdly, God has chosen to use the nation of Israel as a teaching tool to communicate and reveal Himself to the nations of the world, including prophecies about future events (Ex. 14:4 with Rom. 9:17, 1 Sam. 17:46, 2 Kings 19:19, Ez. 38:16-17, Dan. 3:28-29, Dan. 9:24-27, Jer. 23:7-8). That being said, Israel, the apple of God's eye (Zech. 2:8), and Jerusalem, the center of the nations (Ez. 5:5), must play a central role in Bible prophecy.

Gentiles and the New Covenant

God has communicated both the Old and New Covenants in His Word. The Old Covenant was given to Israel at Mt. Sinai (Ex. 20) and the New Covenant is communicated to Israel most clearly in Jeremiah 31:31-34.

> Behold, the days are coming, declares the LORD, when I will make a *new covenant with the house of Israel,* and with the house of Judah: not like the covenant that I made with their fathers on the day when I took them by the hand to bring them out of the land of Egypt, my covenant that they broke, though I was their husband, declares the LORD. For this is the covenant that I will make with the house of Israel *after those days,* declares the LORD, I will put my law within them, and I will write it on their hearts. And I will be their God, and they shall be my people. And no longer shall each one teach his neighbor and each his brother, saying, 'Know the LORD,' for they shall all know me, from the least of them to the

greatest of them, declares the LORD. For I will forgive their iniquity, and I will remember their sin no more *(emphasis mine)*.

Note, however, that this covenant is specifically made with the "house of Israel." So what hope do the Gentiles have? Can those who are not of the house of Israel receive the blessings of this covenant? Praise God, the answer is yes! The simple answer is that all these promises are freely available in Jesus Christ. How do we know this? It is evident in many New Testament passages indicating that salvation is available by God's grace through faith in Christ. One in particular that makes it explicit that the New Covenant extends to Gentiles as well as Jews is Ephesians chapters 2 and 3 (especially Eph. 2:11-19, 3:6). This explains how the apostle Paul can take an Old Testament passage like Hosea 1:9-11, which, in context, was written about Israel, and apply them directly to Gentiles in Romans 9:25-26.

Blinding, Fullness, and Chronology

You may be wondering what this has to do with eschatology. Good question! Romans 9-11 is about Jews and Gentiles coming to faith in Jesus and has some chronology built into it. Romans 9 begins with Paul agonizing over his "kinsman according to the flesh" (Rom. 9:3, *i.e.* Israelites) not believing in Christ. This line of thought concludes in Romans 11 with Paul saying that the Jews of his day had been broken off (Rom. 11:17) of the holy root due to unbelief, being blinded by God so that the gospel and accompanying salvation would go to the Gentiles. At some point, this will provoke the Jews to jealousy, and they will return to God. When will this return of the Jews occur? When the "fullness of the Gentiles" comes in (Rom. 11:25). There is a "full inclusion" of Israel (Rom. 11:12) that is yet to come. It was a future event when Paul wrote the letter to the Romans, and I believe it is still a future event for us as of the writing of this book. Perhaps the phrase "after those days" in the New Covenant text of Jeremiah 31:33 is referring to the days when the fullness of the Gentiles has come in.

Before moving along with the understanding of eschatology, let's talk about this issue of God blinding Israel, cutting off their branches to graft in Gentiles, and then later grafting them back in (Rom. 11:16-25). When Jesus came the first time, He came to the Jews. The gospel came "to the Jew first and also to the Greek" (Rom. 1:16). While the apostles and the first to believe in Jesus at the time were Jews, the nation of Israel as a whole did not receive Jesus as their Messiah. Even to the point of having Jesus crucified on a Roman cross. What they meant for evil, God meant for good (Gen. 50:20)! This can be traced back to the prophecy that God gave to Israel through the prophet Isaiah in Isaiah 6:9-10, which reads:

> And he said, "Go, and say to this people: "'Keep on hearing, but do not understand; keep on seeing, but do not perceive.' Make the heart of this people dull, and their ears heavy, and blind their eyes; lest they see with their eyes, and hear with their ears, and understand with their hearts, and turn and be healed."

8

This prophecy is referenced in Mt. 13:10-16, Mk. 4:10-12, Jn. 12:37-41, Acts 28:24-29. I encourage you to take a moment to read each of these passages and pay careful attention to the context of each. This is the blinding of the Jews that Paul is referring to in Romans 11:7-8.

Notice, however, that this does not mean the Jews cannot believe and be saved during this time period. Romans 11:7 says, "the elect obtained it, but the rest were hardened." Let's understand this correctly in its context. Romans 11:20 makes clear that the blinding of Israel was a judgment resulting from their unbelief. Jesus explains in Mt. 13:15 that their hearts had grown dull, and *they* had closed their eyes. That is, their hard hearts were unwilling to receive the truth.

Jesus spoke in parables to conceal the truths of the kingdom from unbelievers but note that those who received Him by faith could receive these truths and be blessed by them, so there were Jews who did believe in Christ at that time. While the text in John 12:39 says they (the Jews) "could not believe" because of Isaiah's prophecy, it is followed by the statement in John 12:42a, "Nevertheless, many even of the authorities believed in him." How can this be? An explanation is given in 2 Corinthians 3:12-16:

> Since we have such a hope, we are very bold, not like Moses, who would put a veil over his face so that the Israelites might not gaze at the outcome of what was being brought to an end. But their minds were hardened. For to this day, when they read the old covenant, that same veil remains

unlifted, because only through Christ is it taken away. Yes, to this day whenever Moses is read a veil lies over their hearts. *But when one turns to the Lord, the veil is removed. (emphasis mine)*

Note how much of God's grace is found in the word "nevertheless" in John 12:42 and 2 Corinthians 3:16. Even today, while the fullness of the Gentiles is coming in, Jews can still find salvation in Christ when they turn their heart to the Lord through faith in Jesus Messiah. Romans 11:17 says that "some of the branches" were broken off and Romans 11:25 calls it a "partial hardening" that has happened to Israel. Of the local leaders of the Jews that Paul presented the gospel to while under arrest in Rome, Paul says, "some were convicted by what he said, but others disbelieved" (Acts 28:16-31). Paul eve quoted Isaiah 6:9-10 to them during this gospel proclamation. Therefore, in the days from Pentecost to our current time, it is primarily Gentiles who are coming to faith. Jews can still believe as well, but they are just not coming to Jesus in large numbers or as a nation.

While it is true that among believers today "there is neither Jew nor Greek, there is neither slave nor free, there is no male and female: for you are all one in Christ Jesus" (Gal. 3:28), Romans 9-11 makes it clear that in God's prophetic program for the world at-large, there *is* a distinction between Jew and Gentile. Since there is nothing in world history resembling this since Paul's letter to the Romans was written, we can conclude that there is coming a time when these roles will be reversed. At some point in the future, the fullness of the Gentiles will be complete, and the fullness of Israel will follow. Notice that while Galatians 3:28 also says there is "no male and female" the Bible still teaches that there are distinct roles for men and women within the church as well as the home.

Feasts of the Lord

The feasts of the Lord and associated holy days that go with them were given to the nation of Israel to remind them of the mighty works that God has performed for them in the past and His faithful character as well as what He will do for them in the future. These feasts are to be kept annually and Jews are to use them to teach their children about God. These feasts were specifically given to the nation of Israel, but they also teach significant truths about the salvation that is offered through Jesus to all of humanity. As such, they all point to the person of the Lord Jesus, the Messiah. In this sense, these feasts and holy days also have a prophetic significance.

My goal here is not to go into great detail about each feast and what each part teaches, but to give a short summary and illustrate that the first four have been fulfilled specifically on the earth in the land of Israel with the nation of Israel in Jesus Christ.

Fulfilled Feasts

Passover, Nisan 14

The Lord's Passover is defined in Exodus 12:1-14. It was to be observed on the 14th day of the first month of the Jewish calendar year (Nisan, also called Abib) as a memorial of the 10th plague on Egypt and the Exodus of Israel from slavery in Egypt. A male lamb without blemish in its first year was to be selected by each household on the 10th day of the month and killed on the 14th day with its blood placed on the sides and upper posts of the door. The flesh of the lamb was to be roasted with fire and consumed quickly. Anything not eaten was to be burned with fire. According to Exodus 12:12-13, the Lord said,

> For I will pass through the land of Egypt that night, and will strike all the firstborn in the land of Egypt, both man and beast; and on all the gods of Egypt I will execute judgments: I am the LORD. The blood shall be a sign for you, on the houses where you are. And when I see the blood, I will pass over you, and no plague will befall you to destroy you, when I strike the land of Egypt.

The Passover feast not only memorializes the Exodus, but prophetically teaches about the Savior that was to come. Jesus was crucified on the very day of Passover, Nisan 14, in the year AD 30 (Jones, 2009). John the Baptist calls Jesus the Lamb of God, who takes away the sin of the world (Jn. 1:29). John 11:49-52 says the following:

> But one of them, Caiaphas, who was high priest that year, said to them, "You know nothing at all. Nor do you understand that it is better for you that one man should die for the people, not that the whole nation should perish." He did not say this of his own accord, but being high priest that year he prophesied that Jesus would die for the nation, and not for the nation only, but also to gather into one the children of God who are scattered abroad.

14

Notice that the sacrificial death of Jesus on the cross was not just exclusively for the nation of Israel.

The Bible says, "For Christ, our Passover lamb, has been sacrificed" (1 Cor. 5:7b). What is commonly called the Triumphal Entry (Mt. 21:1-11, Mk. 11:1-10, Lk. 19:28-40, and Jn. 12:12-19) can be shown to have taken place on Nisan 10 (Jones, 2009) and corresponds to Jesus Christ as being selected as the Passover lamb. Note how specifically Passover was fulfilled by Jesus, even down to the very day.

Feast of Unleavened Bread, Nisan 15-21

The Feast of Unleavened Bread is very closely tied to Passover. It is a seven-day feast taking place on Nisan 15 through 21 and one of the three times that The Lord calls all Jewish males to come to Jerusalem every year. It is initially defined in Exodus 12:15-20 and is a week that begins and ends with a holy assembly (*i.e.* a sabbath rest) where no leaven can be consumed or kept in the house throughout the week. More details can be found in Exodus 23:15 and 34:18-21, Leviticus 23:6-8, and Deuteronomy 16:16.

In the New Testament leaven is used to describe the pervasive influence of sin in our lives as described in 1 Corinthians 5:6-7:

> Your boasting is not good. Do you not know that a little leaven leavens the whole lump? Cleanse out the old leaven, that you may be a new lump, as you really are unleavened. For Christ, our Passover lamb, has been sacrificed.

Firstfruits, the Day After the First Sabbath After Passover

Firstfruits is defined in Leviticus 23:9-14 and takes place during the Feast of Unleavened Bread because it was to be observed on the day after the first sabbath day (Saturday) that occurs after Passover, meaning that it always takes place on a Sunday. This feast instructs the children of Israel to "bring the sheaf of the firstfruits of your harvest to the priest" (Lev. 23:10).

Following His crucifixion on the 14th day of Nisan, Jesus was resurrected on Sunday, the day following the sabbath day, and also called the first day of the week in the Bible (Mt. 28:1, Mk. 16:9, Lk. 24:1, Jn. 20:1-20). The resurrection occurred on the exact day of the feast of Firstfruits. This is written of in 1 Corinthians 15:20 and 15:23 stating, "But in fact Christ has been raised from the dead, the firstfruits of those who have fallen asleep. ... But each in his own order: Christ the firstfruits, then at his coming those who belong to Christ." The theme of chapter 15 in 1 Corinthians is about the resurrection of Jesus to a glorified body and the subsequent glorification of the bodies of all who believe in Him.

Pentecost, 50th Day After Firstfruits

Pentecost is the second of the three times each year that all Jewish males were to come to Jerusalem and is also called the Feast of Weeks and the Feast of Harvest (Ex. 23:16, Lev. 23:15-21, Deut. 16:16). This feast was to occur on the 50th day after the Feast of Firstfruits, which is the day after the 7th sabbath and, as such, is a Sunday (i.e. the first day of the week). Meat and bread offerings were to be made and called the "firstfruits to the LORD" (Lev. 23:16-17). Additionally, seven lambs, a young bull, and two rams are also to be offered as a burnt offering made by fire. Other offerings are to be made as well and this day is called a holy convocation, which is a sacred assembly in which no work was to be done as in the weekly sabbath.

The fulfillment of this feast is described in Acts 2:1-36 and took place 50 days after the resurrection of Jesus Christ. On this day, the Holy Spirit that Jesus promised in John 14:16-17 was poured out on the devout male Jews that had traveled from "every nation under heaven" (Acts 2:5) and assembled in Jerusalem for the Feast of Pentecost. The concept of firstfruits in the Bible is that the first reaping of a particular harvest were to be offered to God in thanksgiving and in faith that God will bring about the remainder of the harvest. These men were the firstfruits of believers who would be indwelt by the Holy Spirit as Jesus described in John 14:16-17.

Unfulfilled Feasts

Trumpets, Tishri 1

The feast of trumpets is the first of the feasts that occur in the fall. It was to take place on the first day of the seventh month of the Jewish calendar, Tishri (Lev. 23:23-25, Num. 29:1:26). It is described as being "a day of solemn rest, a memorial proclaimed with a blast of trumpets, a holy convocation" (Lev. 23:24). Because Tishri was originally the first month of the Jewish calendar going back to the first month of creation until God changed it to Nisan (also called Abib) at the Exodus from Egypt (Ex. 12:2), this is generally seen as a memorial of creation and an occasion for joy and celebrating (Num. 10:10).

I have wondered if it also might mean that on this day at some point in the future, God will *remember* Israel in the sense that He will bring about the dispensational shift in His attention from Gentiles back to Jews when the fullness of the Gentiles has come in as spoken of in Romans 11. In the context of a scattering (Lev. 26:14-39) of Israel for their sin, Leviticus 26:40-42, 45 states:

> But if they confess their iniquity and the iniquity of their fathers in their treachery that they committed against me, and also in walking contrary to me, and that I walked contrary to them and brought them into the land of their enemies — if then their uncircumcised heart is humbled and they make amends for their iniquity, *then I will remember my covenant with Jacob, and I will remember my covenant with Isaac and my covenant with Abraham, and I will remember the land.* ... But *I will for their sake remember the covenant with their forefathers,* whom I brought out of the land of Egypt in the sight of the nations, that I might be their God: I am the LORD. *(emphasis mine)*

The covenant God is talking about remembering here is not the Old Covenant given to Moses in Mt. Sinai, but the covenant given to Abraham, which is not bound by the Old Covenant. The concepts of scattering and gathering are very important to understanding eschatology and are addressed in the following section. As you will see when we discuss God gathering Israel, another key feature is that God says He will be their God. Notice this is a part of the passage in Leviticus 26:45 as well.

Day of Atonement, Tishri 10

According to Leviticus 16:29-34, Leviticus 23:26-32, and Numbers 29:7-11, the Day of Atonement was to be observed on the tenth day of the seventh month (Tishri 10) and a day to "afflict yourselves." In addition to the prescribed sacrifices, Leviticus 16:32-33 says,

> And the priest who is anointed and consecrated as priest in his father's place shall make atonement, wearing the holy linen garments. He shall make atonement for the holy sanctuary, and he shall make atonement for the tent of meeting and for the altar, and he shall make atonement for the priests and for all the people of the assembly.

This is the one day in the year when an atonement would be made for the entire nation of Israel for the cleansing of their sins (Lev. 16:30,34). As we will see later, mourning, or afflicting one's soul, is associated with the return of the Lord Jesus (Zech. 12, Mt. 24:30, Rev.1:7).

Tabernacles, Tishri 15-22

The Feast of Tabernacles is the last of the three times each year that all Jewish males were to go to Jerusalem and is also called the Feast of Ingathering (Ex. 23:16-17, Ex. 34:22-23, Deut. 16:16). The details of this feast are laid out in Leviticus 23:39-

43 and Numbers 29:12-38. As with all the Scripture references given in this book, I encourage you to go to the Bible, God's holy, eternal, and infallible word, and read for yourself. This feast was to begin on the 15th day of Tishri (the 7th month) and continue for seven days with a special 8th day following that. It was to be a time to "rejoice before the LORD your God" (Lev. 23:40) and dwell in booths to remind them of how God "brought them out of the land of Egypt" (Lev. 23:43). In the description of the new heaven and new earth in Revelation 21, verse 3 says, "And I heard a loud voice from the throne saying, 'Behold, the dwelling place of God is with man. He will dwell with them, and they will be his people, and God himself will be with them as their God'." This feast commemorates God's deliverance of Israel from Egypt and looks ahead to the new heaven and new earth when God will dwell with His people.

Jubilee

Jubilee is not called a feast in the Bible, but it is very significant in its end-times implications. Jubilee was to be observed the year after seven seven-year periods, that is, after seven sabbath years, occurring every 50th year (Lev. 25:8-12). Leviticus 25:10 describes the Jubilee this way:

> And ye shall consecrate the fiftieth year, and proclaim liberty throughout the land to all the inhabitants. It shall be a jubilee to you, when each of you shall return to his property, and each of you shall return to his clan.

Furthermore, servants were to be released (Lev. 25:39-42). The year of jubilee begins on the Day of Atonement and is the only time a trumpet is commanded to be blown on the Day of Atonement (Lev. 25:9). You will find that characteristics of Jubilee are frequently mentioned in prophetic passages.

Scattered and Gathered

Scattering is judgment for Israel's disobedience (Deut. 4:23-26), gathering is blessing out of God's mercy and faithfulness to His covenant with Israel (Deut. 4:31). Scattering and gathering has happened throughout Israel's history, but there will be a final scattering and a final gathering at the end of this world; particularly a gathering out of all the nations where Israel has been scattered. The common themes when Israel is gathered out of the nations are also associated with the Day of the Lord, the Day of Atonement and Jubilee, and the Millennial Kingdom. The connection to these events will be examined in more detail later in this book.

God first revealed the blueprint for the scattering and gathering of Israel in Deuteronomy 4:27-31:

> And the LORD will scatter you among the peoples, and you will be left few in number among the nations where the LORD will drive you. And there you will serve gods of wood and stone, the work of human hands, that neither see, nor hear, nor eat, nor smell. But from there you will seek the LORD your God and you will find him, if you search after him with all your heart and with all your soul. When you are in tribulation, and all these things come upon you in the latter days, you will return to the LORD your God and obey his voice. For the LORD your God is a merciful God.

He will not leave you or destroy you or forget the covenant with your fathers that he swore to them.

The context of this passage sets up a principle to follow as you read through the Bible. Israel's disobedience brings *scattering* and judgment, along with Jews being seen as a curse, a byword, and a reproach among the nations where they are scattered (Deut. 28:37, 1 Ki. 9:7, 2 Chron. 7:20, Jer. 24:9) Now it is clear why Jews are persecuted all over the world. Israel's repentance brings *gathering* and blessing. Though not stated in the passage above, part of the blessing of the final gathering is that Israel will no longer be seen as a curse, a byword, or a reproach among the nations (Isa. 4:1-4, Zeph. 3:19-20), but instead people will seek out Jews because they have heard that God is with them (Zech. 8:23).

Moreover, Deuteronomy 4:30 foreshadows specifically the "tribulation" in the "latter days" and Israel turning to the Lord during that time. Deuteronomy 30:1-10 repeats this principle again and provides more detail. Consider the blessings associated with this mentioning of the Lord gathering Israel:

- God will bring Israel into the land which their fathers (ancestors) possessed, and they will possess it.

- God will do good to Israel, multiplying them even more than in the past.

- God will circumcise their hearts and the hearts of their children to love Him with all their heart and soul.

- God will curse Israel's enemies and those that hated and persecuted them.

- Israel will return to the Lord and obey all His commandments; this is what brings the gathering about and is also a blessing from God that He will empower them to do it.

- God will make Israel prosperous and successful in all their work, including in the fruit of their bodies, livestock, and land.

- God will rejoice over Israel.

These blessings are triggered by Israel's repentance and obedience as a nation and that repentance and obedience is also a blessing in itself. This list of blessings includes elements of the covenant God made with Abraham, such as possession of the land and many descendants (Gen. 15) as well as things like a circumcised heart and the ability to obey God's commandments that are promised in the New Covenant (Jer. 31:33-34). The Abrahamic Covenant is ultimately fulfilled in the New Covenant by faith in Jesus Christ.

God will use the Tribulation period to bring about this New Covenant repentance that will bring about a gathering of Israel. According to Romans 11, Jews, who have been blinded, cast away, and are like olive branches have been broken off because of unbelief, will be grafted back into that olive tree again after the fullness of the Gentiles has come in. The 12,000 virgin male firstfruits in the Tribulation is the beginning of this returning of Israel to God (Rev. 7:3-8, 14:1-5). They are called "firstfruits" because they are the first of the Jewish believers in Jesus Messiah during the future seven-year Tribulation period.

God's desire to gather Israel can be seen in the words of Jesus at His First Coming when He said, "O Jerusalem, Jerusalem, the city that kills the prophets and stones those who are sent to it! How often would I have gathered your children together as a hen gathers her brood under her wings, and you were not willing!" (Mt. 23:37).

In the context of this and the other scattering and gathering passages, where is Israel scattered from and gathered to? It is always the land of Israel, also known as Judea and Samaria throughout the Bible, the land that God gave them through His promise to Abraham (Gen. 12:7, 13:15, 17:18, 15:18-21). It is "the land" that God led them into and gave them after the Exodus.

Jeremiah 23:3-8 speaks of this gathering of Israel from all the countries where God has driven them, listing some of its blessings as well as describing it as such a defining event that people will use it to describe God this way, "Therefore, behold, the days are coming, declares the LORD, when it shall no longer be said, 'As the LORD lives who brought up the people of Israel out of the land of Egypt,' but 'As the LORD lives who brought up the people of Israel out of the north country and out of all the countries where he had driven them.' For I will bring them back to their own land that I gave to their fathers." (Jer. 16:14-15). Jeremiah 23:7-8 repeats this as well. This is the list of blessing from Jeremiah 23:3-8:

- God will bring them to their fold (*i.e.* their own land).

- God will make them fruitful and increase them.

- God will set up shepherds over them to feed them.

- Israel will never live in fear again, nor be dismayed.

- Israel will not lack anything.

- God "will raise up for David a righteous Branch, and he shall reign as king and deal wisely, and shall execute justice and righteousness in the land."

- In the days of this King from David's line Judah shall be saved (relate this to Mt. 24:13) and Israel will dwell safely.

- That King's name will be called "THE LORD OUR RIGHTEOUSNESS" in those days.

Have there already been times in history when Israel has been scattered and gathered? Absolutely. In 721 BC [1] the northern ten tribes were defeated, captured, and deported by the Assyrians (2. Ki. 17:3-6, 1 Chron. 5:25-26). The southern kingdom was carried to Babylon in three deportations in 606, 597, and 586 BC [2] by Nebuchadnezzar's army and Jerusalem was destroyed, including the first temple, which was built under the reign of Solomon (1 Ki. 6).

Jews returned (*i.e.* were gathered) to Jerusalem beginning in 536 BC and rebuilt the city and construction was completed on a second temple in 516 BC [3]. This part of Israel's history is chronicled in the books of Ezra and Nehemiah. The Jewish people were scattered again in AD 70 by the Roman army led by General Titus. Jerusalem was besieged and destroyed again, including the complete dismantling

---

1 Jones, *The Chronology of the Old Testament*, p. 279.
2 Ibid., p. 280
3 Ibid., p. 280.

of the second temple that was prophesied by Jesus in Matthew 24:2.

Significant Old Testament "gather" passages, where the children of Israel are gathered from all nations where God scattered them are listed below. These are not the only verses, but they give a good glimpse into God's future plans for Israel, especially when taken together.

- Deuteronomy 4:27-31
- Deuteronomy 30:1-10
- Jeremiah 23:3-8
- Jeremiah 29:10-14
- Jeremiah 30:3-10, 17-24
- Jeremiah 32:37-44
- Jeremiah 33:6-18, 25-26
- Jeremiah 46:27
- Ezekiel 20:34-38
- Ezekiel 34:11-31
- Ezekiel 36:24-38
- Zephaniah 2:7
- Zephaniah 3:9-20

From our vantage point in human history, it is amazing to consider that the last scattering of Israel from the land God gave them was AD 70 and the next time there was a gathering of Jews to the land occurred in the 20th century, beginning with the Balfour Declaration in 1917 and culminating in statehood for Israel in 1948 following the brutalities they faced in

28

WWII. The story of Israel's return is nothing short of miraculous and unprecedented in history. Today the nation of Israel is thriving economically and is one of the major nations of the world.

Looking forward through the lens of Bible prophecy, there will be a scattering of Israel at the midpoint of the Tribulation and one final gathering at the end of the Tribulation when Jesus returns bodily to the earth. Matthew 24:31 describes this gathering of His elect "from the four winds, from one end of heaven to the other." This will be the fulfillment of Deuteronomy 30:4-5

> If your outcasts are in the uttermost parts of heaven, from there the LORD your God will gather you, and from there he will take you. And the LORD your God will bring you into the land that your fathers possessed, that you may possess it. And he will make you more prosperous and numerous than your fathers.

The Seventy Weeks Prophecy

A good place to begin studying the foundational details of the end times is to understand the "Seventy Weeks" prophecy. This prophecy given by God to the prophet Daniel provides the foundational chronological and thematic framework for the crucifixion of Jesus Messiah and the events that will occur at the end of the age. This important prophecy was given in 539 BC, the first year of Darius of the Medes, near the end of the 70-year captivity which lasted from 606 to 536 BC [4]. It is written in just four verses in Daniel 9:24-27. Let's look at each of these verses one at a time, with a few questions and answers following each.

> **Daniel 9:24** – Seventy weeks are decreed about your people and your holy city, to finish the transgression, to put an end to sin, and to atone for iniquity, to bring in everlasting righteousness, to seal both vision and prophet, and to anoint a most holy place.

In relaying this prophecy to Daniel, the angel Gabriel (Dan. 9:20-23) told him that the seventy weeks would be determined on "your people". The people of Daniel are the Jews. The nation of Israel. The prophecy also says the seventy weeks are determined upon "your city". The city of Daniel is an obvious reference to the city of Jerusalem.

What is meant by "seventy weeks" in Dan. 9:24?

---

4   Jones, *The Chronology of the Old Testament*, p. 280.

The Hebrew word translated as "weeks" here is *shabuwa*`. It is used 20 times in Scripture and is rendered as "week" or "weeks" in 19 of them and as "seven" the other occurrence. It can be used to describe a period of seven days (*e.g.* Ez. 45:21), seven weeks (*e.g.* Deut. 16:9), or seven years (*e.g.* Gen 29:27-30). Which is it here? In this context, 70 weeks of years makes the most sense. The captivity in Babylon during which the prophecy was given was 70 years rather than days or weeks. Also, when you consider the list of things to be accomplished and looking back historically, it must be years.

What is to be accomplished during the seventy weeks? There are six things that will be accomplished:

1. to finish the transgression
2. to put an end to sin
3. to atone for iniquity
4. to bring in everlasting righteousness
5. to seal both vision and prophet
6. to anoint a most holy place

I'm not going to elaborate on these here, but I encourage you to ponder them. The first three items sound like things that were accomplished at the First Advent of Christ, when Jesus was crucified and resurrected, and the last three items sound like things that will be fulfilled at the Second Advent when Jesus returns to the earth.

> **Daniel 9:25** – Know therefore and understand that from the going out of the word to restore and build Jerusalem to the coming of an anointed one,

a prince, there shall be seven weeks. Then for sixty-two weeks it shall be built again with squares and moat, but in a troubled time.

The prophetic time clock for this prophecy begins with the command to restore and build Jerusalem. When did this happen? The commandment to rebuild Jerusalem and its street and wall was given "in the month of Nisan, in the twentieth year of King Artaxerxes" (Neh. 2:1,3,8), which was the year 454 BC [5]. Dr. Floyd Nolan Jones provides a remarkably thorough treatment of the chronology of this along with commentary on the results of several other studies on this matter on pages 205-254 and 300-310 in *The Chronology of the Old Testament* (2009, Jones). You may have a note in a study Bible or have seen other resources on this topic that put this date at 445 BC and mention that the years of the Seventy Weeks prophecy given to Daniel are to contain exactly 360 days each and they refer to them as *prophetic years*. Dr. Jones' work shows that there is no need for this and that ordinary solar years (which contain approximately 365.2422 days each) are to be used when reckoning the time for this prophecy.

"Seven weeks" and "sixty-two weeks" is another way of saying a total of 69 seven-year time periods, which is 483 years. Moving forward from the month of Nisan in 454 BC, 483 years goes to the month of Nisan in AD 30. While it is clear in the Bible that the crucifixion of the Lord Jesus Christ occurred on the 14th day of Nisan on the Jewish calendar, the year has been debated among chronologers and

5   Jones, *The Chronology of the Old Testament*, pp. 236, 254.

scholars. However, Dr. Jones painstakingly provides a compelling case for AD 30 to be year in which the crucifixion of Christ occurred [6].

> **Daniel 9:26** – And after the sixty-two weeks, an anointed one shall be cut off and shall have nothing [7]. And the people of the prince who is to come shall destroy the city and the sanctuary. Its end shall come with a flood, and to the end there shall be war. Desolations are decreed.

When the prophecy refers to Messiah being "cut off," it is speaking about his death, and note that he will "have nothing." This is an appropriate description of Jesus at the crucifixion since soldiers cast lots for his clothing and none of His disciples stayed with Him at that point. The "prince who is to come" is another way of referring to the antichrist. The people of the prince who is to come refers to the Roman General Titus and his soldiers who destroyed Jerusalem and the Temple in AD 70.

> **Daniel 9:27** – And he shall make a strong covenant with many for one week, and for half of the week he shall put an end to sacrifice and offering. And on the wing of abominations shall come one who makes desolate, until the decreed end is poured out on the desolator.

The "he" that is doing the actions in this verse is the "prince who is to come" in the previous verse. He

6   Ibid., pp. 220-240.
7   Other translations say that He will "have nothing" or "have no one." These are also appropriate descriptions of Jesus at the crucifixion since soldiers cast lots for his clothing and none of His disciples stayed with Him at that point.

will confirm [8] the covenant with many for one week. This one week is the 70th week of the Seventy Weeks prophecy. The "many" are commonly understood to be the Jewish people as a nation but could involve other nations with Israel as the focus. The covenant might be some agreement/treaty that is already in existence because the prince that will come will confirm/ strengthen it.

The prince that will come will also "put an end to sacrifice and offering" in the midst of the seven years. For Israel, the sacrifice and oblation refer to the daily sacrifice made by the priests at the temple in Jerusalem. Jesus spoke of this event in Matthew 24:15 as the "abomination of desolation" standing in the holy place, which is in the temple. Notice that around AD 30 Jesus speaks to His disciples about this as a future event and He specifies that it is from the prophet Daniel, who recorded this prophecy in 539 BC. While the temple was destroyed in AD 70 by the Romans, the details of this prophecy are not satisfied. Historically, there is no known covenant confirmed with Israel 3½ years prior to the temple's destruction so it didn't occur in the middle of the 70th week. That means this special seven-year period is still in our future as of the time of this writing.

Remember that each week in this prophecy represents a seven-year period of time. The midst of a week would occur 3½ years into it and leave 3½ years remaining. These two time periods are also identified as "a time, and times, and half a time", forty-two months, or 1260 days. It is understood that "a

8   Or make a strong/firm covenant.

time" is one year, "times" represents two years, and "half a time" is half of a year. Forty-two months also equates to 3½ years and, with 30 days in each of those months, the total number of days is 1260.

- "a time, and times, and half a time"
  - Daniel 12:7
  - Revelation 12:14
- "forty-two months"
  - Revelation 11:2
  - Revelation 13:5
- "1260 days"
  - Revelation 11:3
  - Revelation 12:6

More details of the last seven years of this prophetic time are given in the verses listed above. We will consider each of them and more when we look at the details of The Tribulation.

For 3½ years to be equivalent to 42 months and also 1260 days, it makes sense that time will be measured as 30 days per month, which matches what Genesis 7:11 and Genesis 8:3-4 show in pre-flood days, where 150 days equals exactly 5 months. This is close to today's lunar calendar, which is what the Hebrew calendar is based on and works out to some months having 30 days while others have 29 days for an average of 29.5 days per year. A thirteenth month is occasionally added to realign with solar years. This is a challenging area of study, and some countries today use lunar calendars rather than the Gregorian calendar used by most of the world. Daniel 7:25 says that a future king (the one we call the antichrist - but more on that later) will "think to change <u>times</u> and laws." Whether the world powers use exclusively 30-day months or not, God will use it during the 70th week of this prophecy.

In the last part of Daniel 9:27, it says the conclusion of this prophecy is when "the decreed end is poured out on the desolator." The desolator is the "prince that will come," who is also called the antichrist (1 Jn. 2:22) and the beast (Rev. 13:1-8), and his end is to be thrown into the lake of fire (Rev. 19:20). This will occur at the end of the 70th week of the prophecy and according to the context of Revelation 19:11-21 coincides with the return of Jesus Christ to the earth.

Are the 70 weeks continuous or could there be a time gap between segments? Why are the 70 weeks segmented into 7 weeks, 62 weeks, and 1 week? How can this be explained? Daniel 9:25 speaks of the first 69 weeks as "seven weeks, and sixty-two weeks" (*i.e.* 7 and 62 weeks), but nothing is said in the text about why this is so or that anything specific will occur after the first seven weeks, which is 49 years, from when the commandment is given to rebuild Jerusalem and its streets and walls. There is also no indication that a time gap would occur between the 7th and 8th weeks of the prophetic period. Chronloger and Bible teacher Dr. Floyd Nolen Jones shows that there are exactly 483 years (69 weeks of 7 years each) between the going forth of the commandment to build Jerusalem and the year of the crucifixion of Jesus. [9]

---

9 Jones, *The Chronology of the Old Testament*, p. 236.

However, Daniel 9:26 describes the cutting off of Messiah and the destruction of the city and sanctuary as being *after* the 62-week segment, but not mentioned as being *in* the 70th week. Consider that it will be at the start of the 70th week that the covenant is confirmed with many (Israel) and 3½ years into that seven-year period "he shall cause the sacrifice and the oblation to cease, and for the overspreading of abominations he shall make *it* desolate" (Dan. 9:27). There will need to be time to rebuild Jerusalem yet again and rebuild the temple so that sacrifices can be taking place before the midpoint of that 70th week. Furthermore, the 70th week will end with the "consummation" when the desolator will be judged.

Looking back in history there are no events that coincide with the prophecies of the 70th week. The sacrifices in the temple in Jerusalem were not stopped in AD 33. In fact, careful study of Matthew 24:15, 21, 29-30, 36-44 reveals that Jesus said the abomination of desolation (v. 15) will trigger Great Tribulation (v. 21) and His bodily return to earth will be immediately after that Tribulation (vv. 29-30). He then stresses 3 times that no one knows the day or the hour of His return (vv. 36-44).

Having a time gap in a prophecy is not unique to the Seventy Weeks prophecy. Here are three examples where there does not appear to be a time gap in the original prophecy, but other passages related to it clearly show a chronological gap.

Example 1

Prophecy: Isaiah 61:1-11

Verses 1 and 2 of Isaiah 61 read as follows:

The Spirit of the Lord GOD is upon me, because the LORD has anointed me to bring good news to the poor; he has sent me to bind up the brokenhearted, to proclaim liberty to the captives, and the opening of the prison to those who are bound; to proclaim the year of the LORD's favor, *and the day of vengeance of our God; to comfort all who mourn; (emphasis mine)*

Verses 3 through 11 of Isaiah 61 continue to describe God's future blessings to Israel. You will see later in this book that these are characteristics of the thousand-year reign of Jesus Christ on earth (Rev. 20), which is often referred to by Christians as the Millennial Kingdom.

Related passage: Luke 4:16-21

And he came to Nazareth, where he had been brought up. And as was his custom, he went to the synagogue on the Sabbath day, and he stood up to read. And the scroll of the prophet Isaiah was given to him. He unrolled the scroll and found the place where it was written, "The Spirit of the Lord is upon me, because he has anointed me to proclaim good news to the poor. He has sent me to proclaim liberty to the captives and recovering of sight to the blind, to set at liberty those who are oppressed, to proclaim the year of the Lord's favor." And he rolled up the scroll and gave it back to the attendant and sat down. And the eyes of all in the synagogue were fixed on him. And he began to say to them, "Today this Scripture has been fulfilled in your hearing."

Did you notice that Jesus stopped reading in the middle of a sentence and closed the book? He then announced that that particular scripture was fulfilled. What I placed in italics in the Isaiah 61:1-2 prophecy was not fulfilled during the First Advent of Christ and is much more descriptive of what will occur at the Second Advent of Christ and beyond. The description of Jesus returning to earth in Revelation 19:11-21 sounds like a "day of vengeance."

Example 2

Prophecy: Isaiah 9:6-7

> For to us a child is born, to us a son is given; *and the government shall be upon his shoulder,* and his name shall be called Wonderful Counselor, Mighty God, Everlasting Father, Prince of Peace. Of the increase of his government and of peace there will be no end, *on the throne of David and over his kingdom, to establish it and to uphold it with justice and with righteousness from this time forth and forevermore.* The zeal of the LORD of hosts will do this. *(emphasis mine)*

Related passages: Matthew 1:18-25, Luke 2, Matthew 19:28, 25:31 with Luke 1:32-33

Matthew 1:18-25 and Luke 2 describe the details of the part of this prophecy of a child being born and a son being given. Matthew 19:28 says,

Jesus said to them, "Truly, I say to you, in the new world, when the Son of Man will sit on his glorious throne, you who have followed me will also sit on twelve thrones, judging the twelve tribes of Israel."

40

Similarly, Matthew 25:31 records the words of Jesus saying of Himself:

> When the Son of Man comes in his glory, and all the angels with him, then he will sit on his glorious throne.

You might be wondering what is meant by the "throne of his glory." Consider what the angel Gabriel said to Mary about Jesus in Luke 1:32-33,

> He will be great and will be called the Son of the Most High. And the Lord God will give to him the throne of his father David, and he will reign over the house of Jacob forever, and of his kingdom there will be no end.

His glorious throne is the throne of his father David. Note the timing of when he will sit on it. It will be "in the new world" (Mt. 19:28) when "the Son of Man comes in his glory" (Mt. 25:31). In the context of that passage, this will be at the end of the age, meaning that the part of Isaiah 9:6-7 that has been italicized has yet to occur at the time of this writing. We will take a more in-depth look at this in the section called The Olivet Discourse.

The common thread in the prophecies from Isaiah 9:6-7, Isaiah 61:1-11, and the Seventy Weeks prophecy in Daniel 9:24-27 is that the time gap coincides with the time between the First and Second Coming of Christ, which is commonly referred to by Christians as the church age and the New Testament calls a "mystery" (Col. 1:24-27). The prophesies in Zechariah 9:9-10 fit that pattern as well with the King entering Jerusalem riding a foal of a donkey being fulfilled at the First Coming (Mt. 21:5) and His dominion stretching to the ends of the earth to be fulfilled at His Second Coming (Zech. 14:1-21).

Example 3

Prophecy: John 5:28-29

> Do not marvel at this, for an hour is coming when all who are in the tombs will hear his voice and come out, those who have done good to the resurrection of life, and those who have done evil to the resurrection of judgment.

Related passage: Revelation 20:4-6

> Then I saw thrones, and seated on them were those to whom the authority to judge was committed. Also I saw the souls of those who had been beheaded for the testimony of Jesus and for the word of God, and those who had not worshiped the beast or its image and had not received its mark on their foreheads or their hands. They came to life and reigned with Christ for a thousand years. *The rest of the dead did not come to life until the thousand years were ended.* This is the first resurrection. Blessed and holy is the one who shares in the first resurrection! Over such the second death has no power, but they will be priests of God and of Christ, and they will reign with him for a thousand years. *(emphasis mine)*

Revelation 20:11-15 goes on to describe the judgment of the dead after a thousand-year reign of Christ. Therefore, the resurrection of life and the resurrection of damnation that look like they occur at

42

the same time in John 5:28-29 are actually separated by a thousand years. There is a time gap in the prophecy that can't be seen until more revelation is given in scripture.

Here is one last point about a time gap between the 69th and 70th weeks in this prophecy. Chapter 11 in the book of Romans describes how the nation of Israel has been blinded (which in itself is a fulfillment of a prophecy in Isaiah 6:9-10, 29:10) and therefore cast away, as their branches are broken off of an olive tree, due to unbelief in Jesus Christ [10]. This blindness and casting away is also called a mystery in this passage and is in effect *until* the fullness of the Gentiles comes in, at which time they will be grafted back in (Rom. 11:24-26). It is my contention that the time period between the breaking off of Israel and their restoration is the time gap between the 69th and 70th weeks of the prophecy in Daniel 9:24-27.

---

10 This does not mean that Israelites/Jews cannot be saved today. They certainly can by repentance and faith in Christ (see Jn. 12:37-43, Acts 28:24-28, 2 Cor. 3:12-16), but they are not doing so in large numbers or as a nation like they will be during the 70th week of the prophecy in Daniel 9:24-27.

The Olivet Discourse

The Olivet Discourse is the name people have given to the answers and prophecies Jesus gave to His disciples in the Mount of Olives after they had just walked past the temple in Jerusalem. Jesus told them that that temple would be destroyed. The disciples asked Him about it and what He said in response is recorded in Matthew 24:1-25:46, Mark 13:1-37, and Luke 21:5-37. I strongly urge you to read these passages before you continue reading the rest of this section.

The Olivet Discourse follows an exchange between Jesus and the Pharisees, which Jesus concluded by saying, "For I tell you, you will not see me again, until you say, 'Blessed is he who comes in the name of the Lord'."(Mt. 23:39). Jesus is quoting Psalm 118:26 here and the disciples correctly associate it with the coming of the Messiah. As they pass by the temple and Jesus prophecies that it will be thrown down, Peter, James, John, and Andrew (Mk. 13:3) ask him three questions (Mt. 24:3):

1. When will the temple be thrown down?

2. What will be the sign of Your coming?

3. What will be the sign of the end of the age?

Questions 2 and 3 are related because they occur at the same time. Jesus begins by answering question 3 first (Mt. 24:4-28, esp. 6 & 13-14) and then addresses question 2 (Mt. 24:29-31). *He does not answer question 1.*

Historically, we can look back and see that His prophecy of the temple and surrounding buildings being thrown down was fulfilled in AD 70 when the Roman army utterly destroyed it. When you think about the grand scheme of world events, the temple being thrown down is bad and was extremely important to the Jews but is not nearly as important to the entire world as the Lord Jesus returning in glory to bring this age to an end and set up His kingdom on earth. We can also look at world history and know that up until the time of this writing in 2024, Jesus has not yet returned, and His kingdom has not yet been brought to earth. We as Christians are eagerly awaiting this!

In Matthew 24:4-8, Jesus begins His reply with a warning to not be deceived, particularly by anyone claiming to be the Christ (Messiah). It is evident that He is addressing the question about the end of the age in Matthew 24:6 when He says, "but the end is not yet." This is the passage that calls the following events the "beginning of the birth pains" (Mt. 24:8):

- wars and rumors of wars,
- nation rising against nation,
- kingdom rising against kingdom,
- famines, pestilences, and earthquakes in various places.

The parallel passage in Luke 21:11 adds pestilences and "terrors and great signs" from heaven to this list as well. The word "sorrows" in the KJV translation of verse 8 can also correctly be rendered as birth pains. Why the analogy to birth pains? The events Jesus says will precede His coming have been taking place on the earth since the Fall of man, but at the end of the age, they will get closer together and get more intense and will ultimately culminate in a birth. Other passages use the labor pains analogy to describe this time period as well (see Isa. 66:7-11, Mic. 4:10, 1 Thes. 5:3).

Matthew 24:9-14 doesn't give any specific chronological queues but describes the persecution of Israel (v. 9), more false prophets arising (v. 11), an increase in hatred among people (v. 10 & 12, also see 2 Tim. 3:1-5), and a worldwide preaching of "this gospel of the kingdom" before the end comes (v. 14). In this context, the salvation of the ones who endure to the end is not describing eternal salvation by being born again through faith in Christ, but a physical saving of their lives when Jesus returns to earth at the end of the 70th week of the prophecy given in Daniel 9:24-27. Other passages of Scripture will be shown to bear this out in later sections of this book. Keep reading!

While the immediate context of the Olivet Discourse is that Jesus is speaking *to* Peter, James, John, and Andrew, the words of His reply are recorded for future generations worldwide to read in Scripture. So far, most of the birth pains are described in global terms. Matthew 24:15, however, clarifies the focal point as being the Jews and particularly Jerusalem:

> So when you see the abomination of desolation spoken of by the prophet Daniel, standing in the holy place (let the reader understand).

This verse also connects the signs of the end of the age with the Seventy Weeks prophecy given in Daniel 9:24-27. Jesus said that some point in the future (from His perspective in AD 30), the abomination of desolation that stops the sacrifices in the holy place of the temple in the halfway point of the 70th week will trigger a "great tribulation, such as has not been from the beginning of the world until now, no, and never will be" (Mt. 24:21). The holy place in the temple is the section just on the other side of the veil from the most holy place (Ex. 26:33) and is where the sacrifices take place (Heb. 9:25).

This cannot be speaking of the destruction of the temple by the Romans in AD 70 because there is no known seven-year covenant between Israel and anyone that was confirmed 3½ years prior to the destruction and none of the other details regarding the 70th week of Daniel's prophecy that are given in other verses can be seen to be fulfilled at that time either. This can only mean that a new temple will be built in Jerusalem at some point in the future.

The people that are in Judea when this happens are instructed to flee to the mountains (Mt. 24:16). This is a description of the Jews being *scattered* from Jerusalem. Recall the previous section on Scattering and Gathering and how scattering is a judgment from God. This "great tribulation" is so bad that no human life would survive it unless God shortened the days (Mt. 24:22), so this judgment has a global reach. Fitting this together with the Seventy Weeks prophecy, we can say that these days of Great Tribulation will last for 3½ years.

To arrive at the correct interpretation and remain faithful to the context of the Olivet Discourse, it is important to see the Jewish nature of these descriptions (the temple/holy place, Judea, false Christs/Messiahs) and to recognize that this time

48

period is the fulfillment of the Seventy Weeks prophecy, which specifically has the Jewish people and Jerusalem as its focus.

One of the last things that will occur before Jesus returns in glory is an increase in false Christs and false teachers. According to 1 Timothy 4:1-2 these false teachers will even be people that were once good teachers of the Bible, since they are said to "depart from the faith." These false Christs and false teachers will even have the ability to show great signs and wonders. This deception is spoken of in 2 Thessalonians 2:8-12, which is specifically speaking of the wicked one, the antichrist, after his identity is revealed and he performs signs and wonders using the power of Satan. God turns over those who refuse to receive the truth to fall for this great deception, even giving them a strong delusion leading to damnation.

Looking across the pages of Scripture, we see that signs and wonders have been clustered around the Exodus, the ministries of Elijah and Elisha, the First Coming of Christ, and now we see that God has foretold us that they will be prominent in the lead up to the Second Coming of Christ. Hebrews 2:4 explains that God bore witness to the message of salvation at Jesus' First Coming "bore witness by signs and wonders, and various miracles, and by gifts of the Holy Spirit." The difference in the End Times is that the antichrist and false Christs will be doing the signs and wonders after the working of Satan (2 Thes. 2:9), but nevertheless, it bears witness to their message and God has prophesied it to help people living during those times to not be deceived and to recognize the times.

In Matthew 24:29 Jesus turns to the part of the question about the signs of His coming. Note the chronology of it. It is *"immediately* after the tribulation of those days" (Mt. 24:29). This means that the Great Tribulation is the 3½-year time period that constitutes the second half of the 70th week of the prophecy given in Daniel 9:27, from the time of the abomination of desolation to "the Son of Man coming on the clouds of heaven with power and great glory" (Mt. 24:30).

According to this passage, the sign of His coming appears in heaven, which refers to the sky in this context. It is preceded by the darkening of the sun and moon and the falling of the stars. This makes me think of how the lights are turned off in a theater before a movie or in an auditorium before a concert. The room goes dark to get your attention and to alert you to the fact that the main event is about to begin. Only in this case it is worldwide! The powers of the heavens will be shaken (Mt. 24:29). When the spotlight comes on, you know where to focus your attention.

Verses 30 and 31 of Matthew 24 describe what will happen next:

1. The sign of the Son of man will appear in heaven.

2. All the tribes of the earth shall mourn.

   a. Revelation 1:7 puts it this way:"Behold, he is coming with the clouds, and every eye will see him, even those who pierced him, and all tribes of the earth will wail on account of him. Even so. Amen."

b. Zechariah 12:10-14 foretells a bitter mourning among Jews "when they look on me, on him whom they have pierced."

c. The Day of Atonement is prescribed as a time to "afflict yourselves" (Lev. 23:27-29).

3. All the tribes of the earth will see the Son of man coming in the clouds of heaven with power and great glory.

4. The Son of Man will send His angels with the sound of a great trump to *gather* His elect "from the ends of the earth to the ends of heaven" (Mk. 13:27).

Do you recall the principle of blessings being associated with God gathering His people? There are some tremendous blessings in the Bible that are associated with this gathering. However, before these blessings are instituted, some judgment needs to take place. Jesus inserts emphatic warnings to be ready and to watch and pray in the parables of the fig tree and its leaves, the master watching for a thief, a servant who was left to rule over a household, ten virgins waiting for a bridegroom, and a man traveling to a far country who gave various amounts of talents to his servants (Mt. 24:32 - 25:30). Among these, He also compares His return to the days of Noah in that those who ignored the warnings were taken away by the flood. I'll remind you that the flood was a global event where the unbelievers were removed from the earth and so it will be with the return of the Lord.

After these warnings, Jesus concludes the Olivet Discourse (recorded in Mt. 25:31-46) with a prophecy about what will happen just after He comes in His glory. Jesus, as King over all the earth (Zech. 9:14), will sit on "his glorious throne" (Mt. 25:31), which is a reference to the throne of David in Jerusalem (Lk. 1:32), and will gather all the nations to Himself to separate them "as a shepherd separates the sheep from the goats" (Mt. 25:32). The unrighteous, which correspond to the goats, are sent to eternal punishment and fire (Mt. 25:41, 46) and the righteous, referred to as the sheep, are given eternal life and told to inherit the kingdom that the Father prepared for them from the foundation of the world (Mt. 25:34, 46).

The Olivet Discourse provides important details about the time leading up to the return of Jesus Christ. Believers are to take care not to be deceived, especially by false Christs and false prophets. Believers are to watch, be ready, and pray while we do the work the Lord has given us to do until He returns.

The Tribulation

The 70th week of the prophecy in Daniel 9:24-27 is a seven-year period that is divided distinctly into two 3½-year periods. As previously stated, this "week" has not yet occurred. The 70th week begins when the "prince that shall come" confirms a covenant with many for one week (Dan. 9:27). Daniel 11:21-24 gives more insight into the character of this "prince" and how this covenant will come about by describing him in the following ways:

- he is a contemptible person

- he will come without warning (peaceably)

- he will obtain the kingdom by flatteries

- he will work deceitfully from the time that an alliance made with him

This specific seven-year period is a time when God unleashes a specific series of judgments and wrath on the world in the form of seven seals, seven trumpets, and seven bowls. These are given in a telescoping format in Revelation chapters 6 through 19, with the culmination stated in the sixth seal (Rev. 6:12-17), the seventh trumpet (Rev. 11:15-19), the seventh bowl (Rev. 16:17-21), and the return of the Lord (Rev. 19). More will be said about this later.

As a student of the Word, I'm striving to understand how these events fit together. Sometimes we must make inferences (educated guesses) based on the information given in the Bible. It seems likely to me that it will begin with the confirmation of a covenant with Israel around the time of the fall feasts (Trumpets, Atonement, Tabernacles), the midpoint will be 3½ years later at Passover (I'll explain why in the section on the midpoint of the Tribulation), and it will culminate again 3½ years after that at the fall feasts for a total of seven years. I say this because the first four feasts were fulfilled on each particular day on the Jewish calendar and this would be a way of the final three feasts being fulfilled to the day while still honoring the Scriptures about the 70th week of the Seventy Weeks prophecy being a seven-year period that is divided into two distinct periods.

Like most other aspects of prophecies of the end of the age, the details are found in a variety of passages and must be pieced together by careful study and sticking to Scripture to interpret Scripture. The following sections represent the most likely conclusions regarding the timing of events based on my study of the Bible and the guidance of the Bible teachers and resources that are cited in this work. It will be during this Tribulation time that the fullness of Israel will come in and God will remove their blindness to the gospel (Rom. 11:12, Rom. 11:24-27), which is the culmination of the New Covenant fulfillment in Israel as a nation. God's focus will transfer back from Gentiles to Jews in the 70th week of the prophecy in Daniel 9:24-27, following a long time gap after the first 69 weeks of that prophecy. These first 69 weeks, representing 483 years, began from the "going out of the word to restore and build Jerusalem" (Dan. 9:25) in 454 BC and ended in the year of the crucifixion

54

of Jesus (Messiah cut off, Dan. 9:26) in 30 AD [11]. There are 483 years from 454 BC to 30 AD. Remember that there was no year 0, so the mathematical calculation for the number of years is 454 + 30 − 1 = 483. The feast of trumpets is described as a "memorial" (Lev. 23:24-25, Num. 29:1). Does this mean God will *remember* Israel, His promises to them, and the 70th week of this prophecy? Will this feast be fulfilled with the beginning of the last week of the Seventy Weeks prophecy?

First Half of the Tribulation

Since this is the beginning of the 70th week of the prophecy from Daniel 9:24-27, it will begin with a seven-year covenant/treaty being confirmed between Israel/Jews and the "prince who is to come." This prince will flatter and deceive the Jews with promises of peace during the first 3½ years (Dan. 11:21-24). This fits with the answer Jesus gave Peter, James, John, and Andrew when they asked about signs of the end of the age. The first thing He said was to be careful not to be deceived, particularly by false messiahs (Mt. 24:3-5, Mk. 13:3-6, Lk. 21:7-8).

Two Witnesses

While there will be false messiahs and many false prophets during this time, God will send two true prophets to witness and prophesy during the first 1260 days of the Tribulation (Rev. 11:3). Remember that 1260 days is equivalent to 42 months and also 3½ years when months contain 30 days each. God will protect them and work mighty wonders through them as detailed in Revelation 11:5-6:

11 Jones, *The Chronology of the Old Testament*, p. 236.

> And if anyone would harm them, fire pours from their mouth and consumes their foes. If anyone would harm them, this is how he is doomed to be killed. They have the power to shut the sky, that no rain may fall during the days of their prophesying, and they have power over the waters to turn them into blood and to strike the earth with every kind of plague, as often as they desire.

If the idea of fire proceeding out of their mouths to devour their enemies seems pretty wild, consider the two captains and their 50 soldiers each that were consumed from fire that came from heaven at the words of Elijah the prophet (2 Ki. 1:9-14). Indeed, it could be that the fire actually emanates from their mouths, or it could be that fire consumes these people somehow (from heaven as in 2 Ki. 1:9-14?) when one of the witnesses speaks it, as Elijah did. Similarly, Revelation 19:15 describes a sharp sword that goes out of the mouth of Jesus to strike down the nations and Isaiah 11:4 explains that the Lord will slay the wicked with the breath of His lips.

Again, like Elijah, these two prophets will have the power to prevent rain for 3½ years (1 Ki. 17:1, Jas. 5:17-18). Recall how Jesus also described this time as being characterized by famine (Lk. 21:11). Obviously, droughts and famines go together, which further corroborates that the Olivet Discourse (Mt. 24, Mk. 13, Lk. 21) was about this time period. God will give them power to turn water to blood as He did through Moses as recorded in Exodus 7:17-21 as well as other plagues.

The next few verses (Rev. 11:7-10) describe what will happen to these two witnesses when the 1260 days of their prophecy are complete:

> And when they have finished their testimony, the beast that rises from the bottomless pit will make war on them and conquer them and kill them, and their dead bodies will lie in the street of the great city that symbolically is called Sodom and Egypt, where their Lord was crucified. For three and a half days some from the peoples and tribes and languages and nations will gaze at their dead bodies and refuse to let them be placed in a tomb, and those who dwell on the earth will rejoice over them and make merry and exchange presents, because these two prophets had been a torment to those who dwell on the earth.

The "beast that rises from the bottomless pit" is a description that identifies Satan according to Revelation 20:1-3, 7. With God's permission, Satan is allowed to end the lives of these two witnesses. Perhaps Satan will use the antichrist, who is also referred to as a beast (Rev. 13:1-8) to carry out these murders, since he will be empowering him at this point in time (2 Thes. 2:9). Notice the description of the people of the world to be able to "gaze at" their dead bodies lying in the street of Jerusalem, where Jesus was crucified. At the time this was written that would not have been possible. This may have been difficult to understand in the past, but with today's technology, it is easy to comprehend how that will happen. This is yet another detail of how God is preparing the world today for the End Times events to take place. It also shows us something about how wicked society will be in that the people of the world celebrate the death of God's true prophets.

As the world is making a holiday out of the deaths of these prophets and leaving their dead bodies in the street to rot, God intervenes in a dramatic fashion as described in Revelation 11:11-13:

> But after the three and a half days a breath of life from God entered them, and they stood up on their feet, and great fear fell on those who saw them. Then they heard a loud voice from heaven saying to them, "Come up here!" And they went up to heaven in a cloud, and their enemies watched them. And at that hour there was a great earthquake, and a tenth of the city fell. Seven thousand people were killed in the earthquake, and the rest were terrified and gave glory to the God of heaven.

The 1260-day ministry of these two witnesses corresponds to the first 3½ years of the Tribulation (70th week of Daniel's prophecy) because if it was the second half the 3½ days of the world rejoicing over their deaths and their miraculous resurrection and ascension would occur *after* Jesus returns in person to judge the world at the end of the Tribulation and that just doesn't fit. We will cover that event when we talk about the Day of the Lord in a later section.

The specific identities of the two witnesses are not given in the Bible. Their names are not given. That doesn't keep us from speculating about who they might be, however, and two common theories are that they are Moses and Elijah or Enoch and Elijah. Moses and Elijah because of the nature of the signs and Enoch and Elijah because they are two men that are recorded as being taken to heaven without specifically dying (Gen. 5:24,

2 Ki. 2:11, Heb. 11:5). Notice that Elijah is one of the two in both of these possibilities and fits with Malachi 4:5-6, which says that Elijah the prophet would come "before the great and awesome day of the LORD comes." While this argument is somewhat compelling, remember that John the Baptist came in the "spirit and power of Elijah" (Lk. 1:17) and Jesus said that John was Elijah if the people would receive it (Mt. 11:13-14). Furthermore, Moses and Elijah appeared with Jesus on the mount of transfiguration, which prompted the disciples to ask Jesus why the scribes say Elijah must come first, to which He replied that he *had* come (Mk. 9:2-13). However, John said that he was *not* Elijah (Jn. 1:21).

Yes, this is all a bit confusing, but it does make the point that Elijah himself does not have to actually come back to earth, but that another person could be considered to fulfill that role if they are sent in the spirit and power of Elijah as John was. Whether John would count as Elijah was contingent on whether or not the Jews received him as such.

This is the imagery used to describe the two witnesses in Revelation 11:4, that they are:

- the two olive trees
- the two candlesticks
- standing before the God of the earth

The scenario in Zechariah 4 is a vision given to Zechariah about the rebuilding of the temple under King Zerubbabel after the Jews were released from captivity in Babylon circa 520 to 516 BC. The high priest at the time, Joshua the son of Jozadak, and King

Zerubbabel were over the people in the rebuilding of the temple are described in Zechariah 4:11-14 this way:

> Then I said to him, "What are these *two olive trees* on the right and the left of the lampstand?" And a second time I answered and said to him, "What are these *two branches of the olive trees*, which are beside the *two golden pipes* from which the golden oil is poured out?" He said to me, "Do you not know what these are?" I said, "No, my lord." Then he said, "These are the two anointed ones *who stand by the Lord of the whole earth."* (emphasis mine)

The point here is that these two men could possibly be (in God's view) whoever the rightful high priest and king of Israel are during the first half of the Tribulation. This is just offered as another possibility. The fact is, God doesn't give us their names. He just tells us what we need to know about their ministry.

The 144,000

Revelation 7:3-8 and Revelation 14:1-5 tell us about 144,000 male Jewish virgins, 12,000 from each tribe of Israel, who will place their faith in Jesus. The evidence of this faith in Jesus is that they are said to "follow the Lamb wherever he goes" and are "redeemed from mankind" (Rev. 14:4). They have the name of God, the Father of the Lamb, written on their foreheads (Rev. 14:1) and they have a seal on their foreheads indicating that they are servants of God (Rev. 7:3).

The fact that they are called "firstfruits for God and the Lamb" (Rev. 14:4) is a way of saying that they are the first to believe in a given area or time period (see

60

Rom. 16:5, 1 Cor. 16:15) or, in general, the first of something where more are expected to follow. Based on the placement of these verses and that they are called firstfruits, it is reasonable to conclude that these 144,000 Jews are the first to believe in Jesus Messiah during the Tribulation. That would support the transition spoken of in Romans 11 when Israel, because of their faith, is grafted back into "their own olive tree" (Rom. 11:24) that they had previously been broken off of due to unbelief (Rom 11:20). This change in focus on Gentiles to a focus on Jews is what is meant in Romans 11:12 and 25:

> Now if their trespass means riches for the world, and if their failure means riches for the Gentiles, how much more will *their full inclusion* mean! ... Lest you be wise in your own sight, I do not want you to be unaware of this mystery, brothers: a partial hardening has come upon Israel, until the *fullness of the Gentiles* has come in. *(emphasis mine)*

It is strongly implied that these 144,000 will preach the "gospel of the kingdom" to all nations (Mt. 24:14 with Rev. 7:9) during the Tribulation.

Multinational Attack on the Nation of Israel

Chapters 38 and 39 of the book of Ezekiel foretell the details of a large military force that will attack Israel. These prophecies were written by Ezekiel between approximately 593 and 571 BC. Historically, nothing like what is described in these chapters has ever happened, so obviously they must occur in our future. To see how that might happen, consider what must take place first in the Middle East and what nations must align with each other for this to unfold.

The state of Israel was dismantled by the Roman army in 70 AD. With the destruction of that time and in the centuries to follow, Jews were scattered all over the world. With the Balfour Declaration in 1917 (a formal statement of British support for a Jewish nation in the Middle East) and especially the desire for Jews to return to the land of Israel, biblically known as Judea and Samaria, following World War II, a gathering of Israel in the land God gave them has been underway. By God's grace, Israel became a recognized nation among the nations of the world again in 1948. Historical accounts of how this happened are no less than astonishing, but Ezekiel 38:8 puts it this way:

> After many days you will be mustered. In the latter years you will go against the land that is restored from war, the land whose people were gathered from many peoples upon the mountains of Israel, which had been a continual waste. Its people were brought out from the peoples and now dwell securely, all of them.

Notice all of the details in this one verse. It takes place in the latter years. It specifies that they have been brought back from the sword; just think of what Jews endured during WWII and the years that followed. They are gathered out of many people, meaning that Jews migrated from all over the world to go back to the land of Israel, which has most certainly occurred since WWII. Their land, indeed, has been brought forth out of the nations. This reconstitution of Israel in the land is the beginning of the fulfillment of the prophecy of the dry bones in Ezekiel 37. At this point, the bones have come together and are covered with sinews and flesh and skin, but the breath of God is not yet in them (Ez. 37:7-8).

While they have built up a strong military, it is debatable to say that they "dwell securely" at the time of this writing. However, this will change when the "prince that is to come," whom we also refer to as the antichrist, will confirm a covenant with Israel for seven years, which will mark the beginning of the 70th week of the Seventy Weeks prophecy of Daniel 9:24-27. While it is possible that the events of Ezekiel 38 could take place before the Tribulation, it may be a better fit to think that they will occur in the first half of it when the first two seal judgments are considered (Rev. 6:1-4). We will look at these in detail later.

Who is prophesied to attack Israel in chapter 38 of Ezekiel? Look at Ezekiel 38:2-3,5-6:

> Son of man, set your face toward Gog, of the land of Magog, the chief prince of Meshech and Tubal, and prophesy against him and say, Thus says the Lord GOD: Behold, I am against you, O Gog, chief prince of Meshech and Tubal. ... Persia, Cush, and Put are with them, all of them with shield and helmet; Gomer and all his hordes; Beth-togarmah from the uttermost parts of the north with all his hordes — many peoples are with you.

A coalition of forces involving the nations of Central Asia (Magog), Iran (Persia), Sudan (Ethiopia, Cush), Libya (Put), and Turkey (Togarmah, Gomer) will come to attack the nation of Israel. Moreover, the phrase "chief prince" is translated from the words *ros nasi,* which some English translations render as "prince of Rosh [12]." Many today see Rosh as a reference to Russia and there are historical reasons for this [13]. Ezekiel 38:15 says the leader Gog will come out of the "uttermost parts of the north." Note that Moscow is almost due north of Israel and in the Bible all directions are given with Israel as the reference point. Dr. Andy Woods is an excellent resource for digging into the details of which ancient nations correspond to the nations of today. The connections listed here are from his book titled *The Middle East Meltdown: The Islamic Invasion of Israel* (Woods, 2016).

For several years now Russia and Iran have had a strong alliance and both nations have a military presence in Syria, which borders Israel via the Golan Heights. The other nations involved are Islamic, are on friendly terms with Russia (though this is not always the case with Turkey) and are unfriendly towards Israel. Ezekiel 38:9 and 15 also states that there will be "many peoples" with these nations, so other nations will be involved as well.

While God is ultimately the one bringing this massive army to Israel (Ez. 38:4, 16), it appears the reason for the invasion is that Sheba (Saudi Arabia),

---

12 These include the New King James Version, New American Standard Bible 1995, American Standard Version, Young's Literal Translation, Darby Translation, and the Hebrew Names Version.
13 Andy Woods, Middle East Meltdown 009 Ezek 38v2B-9, *https://cdn.slbc.org/wp-content/uploads/2022/03/05212039/Middle-East-Meltdown-009-Ezek-38v2b-9.pdf* (accessed 19 June 2024).

Dedan (Saudi Arabia or Yemen) and the "merchants of Tarshish" are coming to Israel to "seize spoil" to plunder silver and gold, cattle and goods, and great riches (Ez. 38:13). It appears there are great riches in Israel that they want to take. At the time of this writing, Israel is a very wealthy nation. The stage is being set for this prophecy to come to pass.

Ezekiel 38:16, 23 and 39:6-7 reveal that the ultimate reason for these events is so that the nations will know the Lord, particularly the people of Israel. God will repel this coalition of forces in a dramatic way. Please take a moment to read Ezekiel 38:18 through 39:16 to see the details of how God will use a variety of means to magnificently destroy all but one-sixth of this great army. The devastation will be so great that their weapons will be burned for seven years (Ez. 39:9-10) and specially employed men will spend seven months burying bodies and bone fragments (Ez. 39:12-16).

Before moving on, let's address a couple of points that may lead to confusion when reading Ezekiel 38 and 39. First, while Ezekiel 38:1-39:16 covers events that I believe will take place in the first half of the Tribulation, there is a transition that occurs and Ezekiel 39:17-24 jumps to the end of the Tribulation (compare to Rev. 19:17-18) and Ezekiel 39:25-29 describes the restoration of Israel as they enter into the Millennial Kingdom. It is not unusual for a prophetic passage to cover only the main events that occur over a time period and make no mention of the time in between.

Revelation 20:7-10 describes a battle at the end of the thousand-year kingdom where Satan gathers the nations of the world to surround the believers in Jerusalem. Gog and Magog are mentioned here in the gathering of the nations. I want to clarify that the battle described in this passage in Revelation is not the situation described in Ezekiel 38-39. My intent here is not to present all the reasons why this is so, but to say that just because Gog and Magog are mentioned in both descriptions does not mean that these are the same event.

The Scroll with Seven Seals

Revelation 5 and 6 describe a book (scroll) sealed with 7 seals that is opened by the Lamb, who is the Lord Jesus Christ and the only one worthy to do it. Each seal that is opened reveals judgments that God will execute on the world during the seven years of the 70th week of the Seventy Weeks prophecy. It is difficult to pinpoint exactly how many of these judgments are released in the first half of the Tribulation, but it is a reasonable inference to conclude that the first five seal judgments are opened in it and the remaining judgments delivered in the second half. However, it may be just as reasonable that seals three, four, and five occur in the second half.

Here is a summary of what will happen as revealed by the opening of the first five seals:

- **First seal** – "And I looked, and behold a white horse! And its rider had a bow, and a crown was given to him, and he came out conquering, and to conquer." (Rev. 6:2)

- **Second seal** – "And out came another horse, bright red. Its rider was permitted to take peace from the earth, so that people should slay one another, and he was given a great sword." (Rev. 6:4)

- **Third seal** – "When he opened the third seal, I heard the third living creature say, 'Come!' And I looked, and behold, a black horse! And its rider had a pair of scales in his hand. And I heard what seemed to be a voice in the midst of the four living creatures, saying, 'A quart of wheat for a denarius, and three quarts of barley for a denarius, and do not harm the oil and wine!'" (Rev. 6:5-6)

- **Fourth seal** – "When he opened the fourth seal, I heard the voice of the fourth living creature say, 'Come!' And I looked, and behold, a pale horse! And its rider's name was Death, and Hades followed him. And they were given authority over a fourth of the earth, to kill with sword and with famine and with pestilence and by wild beasts of the earth" (Rev. 6:8)

- **Fifth seal** – "When he opened the fifth seal, I saw under the altar the souls of those who had been slain for the word of God and for the witness they had borne. They cried out with a loud voice, 'O Sovereign Lord, holy and true, how long before you will judge and avenge our blood on those who dwell on the earth?' Then they were each given a white robe and told to rest a little longer, until the number of their fellow servants and their brothers should be complete, who were to be killed as they themselves had been" (Rev. 6:9-11)

Admittedly, I'm speculating that all of the first five seals will be opened and that their content will be carried out during the first half of the Tribulation, but at this time I am not aware of any particular clues to indicate if any of them will take place after the midpoint.

The sixth seal describes the end of the seven years of Tribulation with the culminating event of Jesus Christ returning to judge the earth in person on the Day of the Lord. This seal will be covered in detail later. Remember that these seals are on a scroll with each section describing specific events. The seventh seal contains the descriptions of the judgments that are released by the blowing of seven trumpets (Rev. 8:1-2) and the pouring out of seven bowls of wrath (Rev. 16:1). These will be discussed in the section on the second half of the Tribulation.

A Jewish Temple in Jerusalem

At some point either before the Tribulation begins or during the first half of it Israel will have a functioning temple in Jerusalem. Here are passages that indicate that this must be so.

> **Daniel 9:27** – And he shall make a strong covenant with many for one week, and for half of the week he shall put an end to sacrifice and offering. And on the wing of abominations shall come one who makes desolate, until the decreed end is poured out on the desolator.

This is from the Seventy Weeks prophecy given to Daniel. The sacrifice and oblation referred to are understood to be the offerings made to God at the temple in Jerusalem. Notice that these sacrifices will be stopped for "half the week," which means they will end in the middle of the 70th week of this prophecy. Jesus alludes to this in the Olivet Discourse as follows:

Matthew 24:15 – So when you see the abomination of desolation spoken of by the prophet Daniel, standing in the holy place (let the reader understand).

Jesus is referring to Daniel 9:27 and says that this abomination of desolation will stand in the holy place. The "holy place" is in the temple.

2 Thessalonians 2:4 – Let no one deceive you in any way. For that day will not come, unless the rebellion comes first, and the man of lawlessness is revealed, the son of destruction, who opposes and exalts himself against every so-called god or object of worship, *so that he takes his seat in the temple of God, proclaiming himself to be God. (emphasis mine)*

This passage from 2 Thessalonians is describing future events (even for us still today) and will be covered in more detail when we discuss the antichrist.

Revelation 11:1-2 – Then I was given a measuring rod like a staff, and I was told, "Rise and measure the *temple of God* and the altar and those who worship there, but do not measure the court outside the temple; leave that out, for it is given over to the nations, and *they will trample the holy city for forty-two months." (emphasis mine)*

A temple in Jerusalem, the holy city, will be there during the period of forty-two months, which is a prophetic reference to half of the 70th week of the prophecy in Daniel 9:24-27, also called the seven-year Tribulation. Forty-two months is equivalent to 3½ years.

69

The Antichrist, the Beast, and the Midpoint

There is a man that will be uniquely given over to Satan in the last days. In the Seventy Weeks prophecy given to Daniel he is called "the prince who is to come" (Dan. 9:26). Another name given to this man is given in 1 John 2:22, which reads this way:

> Who is the liar but he who denies that Jesus is the Christ? This is the antichrist, he who denies the Father and the Son.

The words *the* antichrist indicate a unique individual in the same way as the Christ, the Son, and the Father.

The title "antichrist" is first mentioned in 1 John 2:18. In this verse this person is associated with the End Times, referred to as the "last hour." First John 2:18 says:

> Children, it is the last hour, and as you have heard that antichrist is coming, so now many antichrists have come. Therefore we know that it is the last hour

This verse says that the time of the end will be evident when one specific and particular antichrist comes. God has appointed a person for that role in that time. However, there are always many antichrists and John explains in 1 John 4:3 that the spirit of antichrist is one that "does not confess Jesus" and "is not from God."

A key component of the character of the antichrist is given in 1 John 2:22 as he is described as "the liar."

70

Daniel 11:32 describes him as one that will "seduce with flattery those who violate the covenant." He will come "by the activity of Satan with all power and false signs and wonders" (2 Thes. 2:9). While his actions are allowed by God (Rev. 13:5, 7, Rev. 17:17), "his power and his throne and great authority" are given to him by "the dragon" (Rev. 13:1-2), who is Satan (Rev. 12:9).

The beast that rises up out of the sea from Revelation 13:1-4 represents both the antichrist and the global government that he presides over. The principle that a king and his kingdom can be used interchangeably can be seen most clearly in Daniel 2:38-40 where the head of gold in Nebuchadnezzar's dream represents both him and the kingdom of Babylon that he was the king over. Another example, where "the fourth beast" is describing the same beast as in Revelation 13:1-4 is in Daniel 7:7-8, 17-20, where verse 7 says the four beasts are kings while verse 23 says the fourth beast is the fourth kingdom.

The beast of Revelation 13:1-4 is "like a leopard; its feet were like a bear's, and its mouth was like a lion's mouth," meaning that it has characteristics of the kingdoms associated with the kingdoms depicted with those animals in Daniel 7:1-6. Looking back in history to the time of Daniel, it is known that the kingdom of Babylon was the dominant power on earth at the time of Daniel and was followed by the kingdoms of Medo-Persia (Dan. 5:28) and Greece (Dan. 8:20-21). The leopard represents Greece, the bear represents the Medo-Persian empire, and the lion must represent the Babylonian kingdom under Nebuchadnezzar. The fourth beast in Daniel 7 corresponds to the Roman

Empire, which followed the Grecian Empire, but is ultimately fulfilled by the future global kingdom of the antichrist, which will have characteristics of each of the previous kingdoms but will also be different from them, more dreadful, and will devour the whole earth (Dan. 7:7, 19, 23).

This beast is described as having seven heads (Rev. 13:1). Revelation 17:9-11 says these heads are seven mountains. A mountain is another biblical metaphor for a kingdom. At the time John wrote the book of Revelation, he said of the seven kings over these kingdoms in Revelation 17:10-11:

> They are also seven kings, five of whom have fallen, one is, the other has not yet come, and when he does come he must remain only a little while. As for the beast that was and is not, it is an eighth but it belongs to the seven, and it goes to destruction.

Tracing kingdoms in the Bible, the five that have fallen are Egypt, Assyria, Babylon, Medo-Persia, and Greece, in that order. The kingdom that was current in John's day was the Roman Empire. A seventh kingdom will rule and then an eighth kingdom will arise and be the final beast and will actually be of the first seven.

This beast is also described as having ten horns (Rev. 13:1). A horn in the bible represents an authority figure. Revelation 17:12-13 describes these horns this way:

> And the ten horns that you saw are ten kings who have not yet received royal power, but they are to receive authority as kings for one hour,

72

together with the beast. These are of one mind, and they hand over their power and authority to the beast.

There is yet another horn in addition to the ten that is described as follows:

Daniel 7:8 – I considered the horns, and behold, there came up among them another horn, a little one, before which three of the first horns were plucked up by the roots. And behold, in this horn were eyes like the eyes of a man, and a mouth speaking great things.

Daniel 7:20-21 – And about the ten horns that were on its head, and the other horn that came up and before which three of them fell, the horn that had eyes and a mouth that spoke great things, and that seemed greater than its companions. As I looked, this horn made war with the saints and prevailed over them.

Daniel 7:24-25 – As for the ten horns, out of this kingdom ten kings shall arise, and another shall arise after them; he shall be different from the former ones, and shall put down three kings. He shall speak words against the Most High, and shall wear out the saints of the Most High, and shall think to change the times and the law; and they shall be given into his hand for a time, times, and half a time.

This little horn is the antichrist. The beast. The son of perdition. The man of lawlessness. Daniel 11:37 has this to say about him:

He shall pay no attention to the gods of his fathers, or to the one beloved by women. He shall not pay attention to any other god, for he shall magnify himself above all.

The following list contains names and character traits of the antichrist.

- Beast (Dan. 7:17-20, Rev. 13:1-4, 18)
- Man of lawlessness, son of destruction, lawless one (2 Thes. 2:3, 8)
- Among 10 horns (Dan. 7:7, 19-20, 24, Rev. 13:1-3, Rev. 17:12-13, 16)
- Little horn (Dan, 7:8, Dan. 8:9)
- King of bold face (Dan. 8:23)
- The prince who is to come (Dan. 9:26)
- Confirms the covenant with many for 7 years (Dan. 9:27)
- Exalts himself, speaks against God (Dan. 7:8, Dan. 8:10-11, 25, Dan. 11:36-37, 2 Thes. 2:4)
- Devours the whole earth (Dan. 7:23, Rev. 13:7)
- Takes away the daily sacrifice at the midpoint of 7-year covenant (Dan. 8:11-12, Dan. 9:27, Dan. 11:31, 2 Thes. 2:4)
- Makes war with saints for 42 months (Dan. 7:25, Dan. 8:13-14, Dan. 12:7, Rev. 13:5, 7-8)
- Empowered by Satan (Dan. 8:24, Dan. 11:39, 2 Thes. 2:9, Rev. 13:2)
- Allowed by God (Rev. 13:5, 7, Rev. 17:12, 17)
- At the time of the end (Dan. 8:17, 19, Dan, 11:35)

Second Thessalonians 2:1-12 provides a number of key details about what will happen at the end of the age. This passage begins with references to (1) "the coming of our Lord Jesus Christ," (2) "our being gathered together to him," and (3) the "day of the Lord." In the same way that Jesus warned of deception as a sign of the end of the age (Mt. 24:4-5, 24), Paul exhorts the Thessalonians not to be shaken in mind or alarmed (2 Thes. 2:2) and then in 2 Thessalonians 2:3 says:

> Let no one deceive you in any way. For that day will not come, unless the rebellion comes first, and the man of lawlessness is revealed, the son of destruction.

In other words, the day of the Lord (which we will discuss later) shall not come until after there is first a rebellion and the revealing of the man of lawlwssness, who is the antichrist. How can we know that this is a reference to the antichrist? Because the next verse (2 Thes. 2:4) describes him this way:

> Who opposes and exalts himself against every so-called god or object of worship, so that he takes his seat in the temple of God, proclaiming himself to be God.

This is the attitude of the antichrist as he is described as the little horn and king of fierce countenance in Daniel 7:8, 8:9-11, 23-25 (also see Dan 11:36). Considering 2 Thessalonians 2:4 in light of Daniel 9:27 and Matthew 24:15 means that this abomination in the temple will interrupt the sacrifices that will be taking place at the time and will occur halfway through the 70th week of the Seventy Weeks prophecy, which is the seven-year Tribulation. This also implies that a functioning temple must also be standing in Jerusalem at the time and so at some point between now and then that temple must be built.

In the first half of the seven-year Tribulation the antichrist will "come in without warning, and obtain the kingdom by flatteries" (Dan. 11:21) but then will change tactics at the midpoint, when he will "put an end to sacrifice and offering" (Dan. 9:27), and declare himself to be worshiped as if he was God (2 Thes. 2:4). At this point he will also unleash a persecution of Jews (Mt. 24:16-22) and the saints (Dan. 7:21, 25, Rev. 13:7), that is, those who place their faith in Jesus Christ. This will be discussed in more detail in the next section.

In his pride, Satan has always wanted to be in God's place (Ez. 28:2) and likes to mimic but also pervert God's ways. Since God is a triune being, that is, three persons in one being, Satan considers himself as though he is God the Father and that this human antichrist is like Jesus Christ, the son of God. In the next section we will discuss another beast from Revelation known as the false prophet, who Satan will attempt to use in the capacity of the Holy Spirit. We can consider Satan, the antichrist, and the false prophet to be an unholy trinity.

As Jesus the true Messiah experienced death and was resurrected, Satan has his fake messiah antichrist experience a death and resurrection as well (Rev. 13:4, 14). Jesus was killed by crucifixion. Satan perverts the method of death by having his antichrist killed by a head wound made with a sword. This brings up questions about the power that God allows Satan to have during this time or if the death and resurrection were actually legitimate or some kind of trick, but I am not going to explore that in this book. However, there may be a chronological clue in this. If Satan is trying to supplant the sacrifice and resurrection of Jesus with a sacrifice and resurrection of his antichrist, maybe he will coordinate it to occur on Passover (*i.e.* spring). If this occurs in the *middle* of the seven-year Tribulation period, then 3½ years in either direction will mean the beginning and end of the Tribulation will occur in the fall, around the time of the fall feasts.

In the midpoint of the 70th week of the Seventy Weeks prophecy, this seven-year Tribulation period, the antichrist will also cause the sacrifices at the temple to cease (Dan. 9:27, Mt. 24:15) and begin a vicious persecution of the Jewish people, beginning in the land of Israel. This is the warning Jesus gives in the Olivet Discourse when he says to those in Judea to flee to the mountains immediately, not even stopping to take anything from their houses. Jesus says that this is the beginning of the "great tribulation, such as has not been from the beginning of the world until now, no, and never will be" (Mt. 24:21). Jews have been scattered many times as a judgment from God throughout history but will be dramatically scattered from Judea one last time in the middle of the Tribulation.

Second Half of the Tribulation

As we just discussed in the previous section, a lot of major events will occur at the midpoint of the seven-year Tribulation period. For the first 3½ days of this 3½-year period that will be the second half of the Tribulation, people all over the world will be celebrating the death of the two witnesses. This is how Revelation 11:11-13 describes what will happen at the end of the 3½ days:

> But after the three and a half days a breath of life from God entered them, and they stood up on their feet, and great fear fell on those who saw them. Then they heard a loud voice from heaven saying to them, "Come up here!" And they went up to heaven in a cloud, and their enemies watched them. And at that hour there was a great earthquake, and a tenth of the city fell. Seven thousand people were killed in the earthquake, and the rest were terrified and gave glory to the God of heaven.

While it looks hopeful that some people gave glory to God as a result of the ascension of these two prophets, the second half of the Tribulation is identified by Jesus as a time of "great tribulation" that is worse than any other time in history and that if God doesn't cut those days short, no human being will survive them (Mt. 24:21-22).

Antichrist's Persecution of the Saints

Revelation 13:5 says that the beast (*i.e.* antichrist) will be given authority for 42 months. He will use this authority to persecute those who place their faith in Jesus Christ. Here are some relevant verses that summarize how the beast will use the authority that God will allow him to have under the power of Satan during the second half of the Tribulation:

78

Revelation 13:7 – Also it was allowed to make war on the saints and to conquer them. And authority was given it over every tribe and people and language and nation.

Daniel 7:21– As I looked, this horn made war with the saints and prevailed over them.

Daniel 7:25 – He shall speak words against the Most High, and shall wear out the saints of the Most High, and shall think to change the times and the law; and they shall be given into his hand for a time, times, and half a time.

Daniel 8:23-25 – And at the latter end of their kingdom, when the transgressors have reached their limit, a king of bold face, one who understands riddles, shall arise. His power shall be great — but not by his own power; and he shall cause fearful destruction and shall succeed in what he does, and destroy mighty men and the people who are the saints. By his cunning he shall make deceit prosper under his hand, and in his own mind he shall become great. Without warning he shall destroy many. And he shall even rise up against the Prince of princes, and he shall be broken — but by no human hand.

Daniel 12:7 – And I heard the man clothed in linen, who was above the waters of the stream; he raised his right hand and his left hand toward heaven and swore by him who lives forever that it would be for a time, times, and half a time, and that when the shattering of the power of the holy people comes to an end all these things would be finished.

> **Luke 21:22-24** – For these are days of vengeance, to fulfill all that is written. Alas for women who are pregnant and for those who are nursing infants in those days! For there will be great distress upon the earth and wrath against this people. They will fall by the edge of the sword and be led captive among all nations, and Jerusalem will be trampled underfoot by the Gentiles, until the times of the Gentiles are fulfilled.

This great persecution of Jews and all who believe in Jesus Christ (*i.e.* saints) will become very intense at the beginning of the second half of the Tribulation. The antichrist will take control of the rebuilt temple in Jerusalem during the 42-month duration of this Great Tribulation (Rev. 11:1-2).

Eventually in the second half of the Tribulation, Jerusalem will be surrounded by armies from all nations and two-thirds of the population of Israel will be killed (Zeph. 3:8, Zech. 12:2-3, 13:8-9, 14:2). Of the remaining third of the Jews, Zechariah 13:9 says:

> And I will put this third into the fire, and refine them as one refines silver, and test them as gold is tested. They will call upon my name, and I will answer them. I will say, 'They are my people'; and they will say, 'The LORD is my God.'"

In Luke's account of the Olivet Discourse, Luke 21:20-24 records Jesus' description of the attack on Jerusalem, which will occur at the midpoint of the Tribulation, and what will follow in the second half of the Tribulation this way:

80

But when you see Jerusalem surrounded by armies, then know that its desolation has come near. Then let those who are in Judea flee to the mountains, and let those who are inside the city depart, and let not those who are out in the country enter it, for these are days of vengeance, to fulfill all that is written. Alas for women who are pregnant and for those who are nursing infants in those days! For there will be great distress upon the earth and wrath against this people. They will fall by the edge of the sword and be led captive among all nations, and Jerusalem will be trampled underfoot by the Gentiles, until the times of the Gentiles are fulfilled.

For clarification, the "times of the Gentiles" in Luke 21:24 corresponds to the Gentile control of Jerusalem and the Temple court described in Revelation 11:2 but is not the same as the "fullness of the Gentiles" described in Romans 11:25. According to their respective contexts, the times of the Gentiles is a negative thing and refers to the dominating and defiling the holy city of Jerusalem until the end of the Tribulation, and especially during the second half of it. On the other hand, the fullness of the Gentiles is a positive thing and is a label for all the Gentiles that God will save prior to the Rapture of the church, at which time His focus will return to Israel and He will remove their blindness regarding Jesus the Savior.

The False Prophet

It is also at this point that the religious aspect of this global system will intensify as well. As part of Satan's unholy trinity, Revelation 13:11-17 describes a beast that comes up out of the earth who is described as:

- having two horns like a lamb and speaking as a dragon (Satan),

- having the same power as the beast from the sea (the antichrist),

- causing the people of the earth to worship the antichrist,

- performing great signs, including making fire come down from heaven,

- deceiving people on earth through miracles,

- giving "life" to an image of the beast that can speak,

- killing anyone that refuses to worship the image of the beast,

- endeavoring to cause everyone on earth to receive the mark of the beast in/on their right hand or forehead (the Greek can be either "in" or "on" here),

- and preventing anyone without the mark from buying or selling anything.

With the technology available in our world today, including artificial intelligence, it's not hard to see how this kind of control over people will be accomplished worldwide.

Revelation 19:20 refers to this beast as the "false prophet" and from the description in Revelation 13:11-17 he has been given the ability to perform miraculous signs and wonders. Recall the words of warning Jesus spoke in the Olivet Discourse about not being deceived and being wary of false Christs and false prophets (Mt. 24:4-5, 23-24). He was prophesying about this Great Tribulation time period. God has given these warnings in the Bible so that the people living during that time might not be deceived.

Globalism Under Satan

The second half of the Tribulation will be characterized by three areas of globalism: global government under the tyranny of the antichrist (Rev. 13:7), global religion under the tyranny of the false prophet (Rev. 13:12-15), and a global economy under the control of both (Rev. 13:16-17). Daniel 7:23 describes it this way:

> Thus he said: "As for the fourth beast, there shall be a fourth kingdom on earth, which shall be different from all the kingdoms, and it shall devour the whole earth, and trample it down, and break it to pieces."

The headquarters for these three global systems will be centered in the city of Babylon in modern day Iraq (Rev. 17-18). Babylon is described as a "woman" sitting on top of the beast (Rev. 17:3), the great city (Rev. 17:10) that will make the merchants of the earth rich, including trading in slaves and the souls of men (Rev. 18:11-13). She will reign over the kings of the earth (Rev. 17:18) and will deceive the nations of the earth by her "sorcery" (Rev. 18:23). The English word "sorcery" is translated from the Greek word *pharmakeia*. Does that look familiar? It is also the root word for pharmaceuticals! This is not to say that pharmaceuticals are bad in and of themselves, but the point is that they can be used very powerfully by evil people and by Satan to deceive, injure, control, and kill people. This future Babylon will also be known for how it persecutes believers in that she is "drunk with the blood of the saints, and with the blood of the martyrs of Jesus" (Rev. 17:6).

Babylon will be the center for the global economy and is also called the "mother of prostitutes and of earth's abominations" (Rev. 17:5). The false religions of the world can be traced back to the tower of Babel in the land of Shinar (another name for Babylon). These "prostitutes" that this woman is the mother of represent the false religions of the world. In the Tribulation, Babylon will be the mother of "the great prostitute who is seated on many waters" (Rev. 17:1), which will be the global false religion of that time (Rev. 17:15). The effect of this global religion is that with this great whore "the kings of the earth have committed sexual immorality, and with the wine of whose sexual immorality the dwellers on earth have become drunk" (Rev. 17:2). The kings of the earth are the people with the authority; those who rule over nations. Fornication (in Greek, *porneuo*) includes every kind of sexual sin. This global false religion will be intermingled with government as well as commerce and will have sexual sin as a primary characteristic.

While the global false religion will help to build the kingdom of the beast, it won't last through the entire seven years of the Tribulation period. The ten kings that receive power with the beast (Rev. 17:2) will hate this false religion, which is referred to as "the prostitute" and will "make her desolate and naked, and devour her flesh, and burn her up with fire" (Rev. 17:16). The city of Babylon, the center of the global economy and called "the woman" in Revelation 17 and 18, will also not make it to the end of the Tribulation. In this case, God will bring the judgment directly (Rev. 18:8). Revelation 18 is dedicated to describing how the city will be destroyed and burned with fire in one day and how the kings and merchants of the earth will mourn and weep over it. On the other hand, there will be rejoicing in heaven because God will have avenged the apostles, prophets, and all the saints that were killed because of the evil and deception coming out of Babylon (Rev. 18:20-24).

The Seventh Seal

In the Old Testament, the prophet Jeremiah under the inspiration of the Holy Spirit called the Tribulation time "the time of distress for Jacob" and said that there will be no other time like it and likened it to a woman in labor (Jer. 30:6-7). In the New Testament, Jesus also uses the analogy of birth pains to describe this time (Mt. 24:8). In the same way that labor contains birth pains that increase in frequency and intensity until the birth, the seventh seal from the seven-sealed scroll that Jesus Christ was given to open contains the description of seven angels that are given seven trumpets and seven bowls that will release more of God's judgments on the earth with increasing frequency and intensity until the day Jesus physically returns to judge the earth in person (Rev. 8-11, 15-16).

The judgments brought on by the sounding of the first 6 trumpets are described this way in the Bible.

- **First Trumpet** – "The first angel blew his trumpet, and there followed hail and fire, mixed with blood, and these were thrown upon the earth. And a third of the earth was burned up, and a third of the trees were burned up, and all green grass was burned up" (Rev. 8:7)

- **Second Trumpet** – "The second angel blew his trumpet, and something like a great mountain, burning with fire, was thrown into the sea, and a third of the sea became blood. A third of the living creatures in the sea died, and a third of the ships were destroyed" (Rev. 8:8-9)

- **Third Trumpet** – "The third angel blew his trumpet, and a great star fell from heaven, blazing like a torch, and it fell on a third of the rivers and on the springs of water. The name of the star is Wormwood. A third of the waters became wormwood, and many people died from the water, because it had been made bitter" (Rev. 8:10-11)

- **Fourth Trumpet** –"The fourth angel blew his trumpet, and a third of the sun was struck, and a third of the moon, and a third of the stars, so that a third of their light might be darkened, and a third of the day might be kept from shining, and likewise a third of the night" (Rev. 8:12)

The Fifth Trumpet releases special locusts from the abyss (bottomless pit) that sting people like scorpions. The sting does not kill, but torments whoever is stung for five months with pain so severe that they wish for death but it does not come. These locusts are directed not to hurt those that have the seal of God in their foreheads (*i.e.* the 144,000) nor any green plant (Rev. 9:1-12). Next, the Sixth Trumpet releases four angels who are bound in the Euphrates River. These angels bring an army of 200 million horsemen on special horses that kill one-third of the people on earth through fire, smoke, and sulfur coming from their mouths. They also have tails that have heads like snakes that hurt people as well (Rev. 9:13-21).

Likewise, the judgments brought on by the pouring out of the first six bowls are described as follows in the Bible.

- **First Bowl** – "So the first angel went and poured out his bowl on the earth, and harmful and painful sores came upon the people who bore the mark of the beast and worshiped its image" (Rev. 16:2).

- **Second Bowl** – "The second angel poured out his bowl into the sea, and it became like the blood of a corpse, and every living thing died that was in the sea" (Rev. 16:3).

- **Third Bowl** – "The third angel poured out his bowl into the rivers and the springs of water, and they became blood" (Rev. 16:4).

- **Fourth Bowl** – "The fourth angel poured out his bowl on the sun, and it was allowed to scorch people with fire. They were scorched by the fierce heat, and they cursed the name of God who had power over these plagues. They did not repent and give him glory" (Rev. 16:8-9).

- **Fifth Bowl** – "The fifth angel poured out his bowl on the throne of the beast, and its kingdom was plunged into darkness. People gnawed their tongues in anguish and cursed the God of heaven for their pain and sores. They did not repent of their deeds" (Rev. 16:10-11).

- **Sixth Bowl** – "The sixth angel poured out his bowl on the great river Euphrates, and its water was dried up, to prepare the way for the kings from the east. And I saw, coming out of the mouth of the dragon and out of the mouth of the beast and out of the mouth of the false prophet, three unclean spirits like frogs. For they are demonic spirits, performing signs, who go abroad to the kings of the whole world, to assemble them for battle on the great day of God the Almighty. … And they assembled them at the place that in Hebrew is called Armageddon" (Rev. 16:12-14,16).

Mercy in the Midst of Judgment

While the symbolism of a woman in Revelation 18 is referring to the city of Babylon, another woman is spoken of in Revelation 12 that symbolizes the nation of Israel. This is clear because it says that "she gave birth to a male child, one who is to rule all the nations with a rod of iron, but her child was caught up to God and to his throne" (Rev. 12:5). Jesus took on human flesh as an Israelite, being born in the tribe of Judah and after His crucifixion and resurrection He ascended into heaven (Acts 1:9-11) and is seated with God on His throne (Rev. 3:21). As we have covered already, the Jews will suffer intense persecution from the beast particularly during the second half of the Tribulation. God will provide protection for them during this time. Consider what Revelation 12:6 says about what God will do for this woman that symbolizes Israel:

> And the woman fled into the wilderness, where she has a place prepared by God, in which she is to be nourished for 1,260 days.

Notice the length of the time frame of 1260 days here. This is equivalent to 42 months with 30 days per month, which is also called a time, times, and half a time - another way of saying 3½ years. This fits best to view it as the second half of the 7 years that make up the 70th week of the prophecy in Daniel 9:24-27. Also consider how the woman fleeing into the wilderness is another way of saying what Jesus described in the Olivet Discourse when He directs people in Judea who see the abomination of desolation in the holy place and Jerusalem surrounded to flee to the mountains (Mt. 24:16, Lk. 21:21).

Continuing in Revelation 12, verses 7 through 12 describe a war in heaven where Michael and his angels will fight against Satan (the dragon) and his fallen angels. The result will be that Satan and the angels devoted to him are cast out of heaven into the earth. This will make Satan very angry and even though he knows he will have only a short time left, he will seek to unleash his wrath on the nation of Israel as well as anyone who trusts in Jesus for salvation. Here is how it is described in Revelation 12:13-17:

> And when the dragon saw that he had been thrown down to the earth, he pursued the woman

who had given birth to the male child. But the woman was given the two wings of the great eagle so that she might fly from the serpent into the wilderness, to the place where she is to be nourished for a time, and times, and half a time. The serpent poured water like a river out of his mouth after the woman, to sweep her away with a flood. But the earth came to the help of the woman, and the earth opened its mouth and swallowed the river that the dragon had poured from his mouth. Then the dragon became furious with the woman and went off to make war on the rest of her offspring, on those who keep the commandments of God and hold to the testimony of Jesus. And he stood on the sand of the sea.

God mercifully provides protection for Israel during this time of persecution.

Out of His great lovingkindness, grace, and mercy God also provides yet another warning to the people of the world at that time by having an angel fly through the sky "with an eternal gospel to proclaim to those who dwell on earth, to every nation and tribe and language and people" and proclaiming, "Fear God and give him glory, because the hour of his judgment has come, and worship him who made heaven and earth, the sea and the springs of water" (Rev. 14:6-7).

The sixth seal, seventh trumpet, and seventh bowl all describe the same event, which is the Second Coming of the Lord Jesus to judge the earth and establish His kingdom here. This is the beginning of the Day of the Lord in Scripture and will be covered next.

The Day of the Lord

The Day of the Lord is the culmination of the seven-year Tribulation period and is when Jesus Christ will return with all His angels and saints to the earth to execute judgment on all who reject Him, physically save those who trust in Him, and set up His kingdom that will rule over all the earth. The Day of the Lord marks "the end of the age" (Mt. 13:39, 49, Mt. 24:3, Mt. 28:20) and includes "the age to come" (Mt. 12:32, Mk. 10:30, Lk. 18:30). In this section, we will examine the details of the Day of the Lord that are given in the Bible.

Depictions in the Old Testament

Let's begin by looking at the portrayals of the Day of the Lord in the Old Testament. Reading through them gives a sense of the bigger picture. Old Testament prophecies often have a near (partial) fulfillment and also a far (ultimate) fulfillment, so the present and the future are somewhat mingled together. Keep this in mind as you consider the broader context of each of the following passages. Also remember that when LORD is in all capital letters, it is the English tetragrammaton YHWH (*i.e.* Yahweh, Jehovah) of the Hebrew word for God in the Bible.

> **Isaiah 2:11-21** – The haughty looks of man shall be brought low, and the lofty pride of men shall be humbled, and the LORD alone will be

exalted in that day. For the LORD of hosts has a day against all that is proud and lofty, against all that is lifted up — and it shall be brought low; against all the cedars of Lebanon, lofty and lifted up; and against all the oaks of Bashan; against all the lofty mountains, and against all the uplifted hills; against every high tower, and against every fortified wall; against all the ships of Tarshish, and against all the beautiful craft. And the haughtiness of man shall be humbled, and the lofty pride of men shall be brought low, and the LORD alone will be exalted in that day. And the idols shall utterly pass away. And people shall enter the caves of the rocks and the holes of the ground, from before the terror of the LORD, and from the splendor of his majesty, when he rises to terrify the earth. In that day mankind will cast away their idols of silver and their idols of gold, which they made for themselves to worship, to the moles and to the bats, to enter the caverns of the rocks and the clefts of the cliffs, from before the terror of the LORD, and from the splendor of his majesty, when he rises to terrify the earth.

Isaiah 13:4-13 – The sound of a tumult is on the mountains as of a great multitude! The sound of an uproar of kingdoms, of nations gathering together! The LORD of hosts is mustering a host for battle. They come from a distant land, from the end of the heavens, the LORD and the weapons of his indignation, to destroy the whole land. Wail, for the day of the LORD is near; as destruction from the Almighty it will come! Therefore all hands will be feeble, and every human heart will melt. They will be dismayed: pangs and agony will seize them; they will be in anguish like a woman in labor. They will look aghast at one another; their faces will be aflame. Behold, the day of the LORD comes, cruel, with wrath and fierce anger, to make the land a desolation and to destroy its sinners from it. For the stars of the heavens and their constellations will not give their light; the sun will be dark at its rising, and the moon will not shed its light. I will punish the world for its evil, and the wicked for their iniquity; I will put an end to the pomp of the arrogant, and lay low the pompous pride of the ruthless. I will make people more rare than fine gold, and mankind than the gold of Ophir. Therefore I will make the heavens tremble, and the earth will be shaken out of its place, at the wrath of the LORD of hosts in the day of his fierce anger.

Joel 2:31-32 – The sun shall be turned to darkness, and the moon to blood, before the great and awesome day of the LORD comes. And it shall come to pass that everyone who calls on the name of the LORD shall be saved. For in Mount Zion and in Jerusalem there shall be those who escape, as the LORD has said, and among the survivors shall be those whom the LORD calls.

Joel 3:11-17 – Hasten and come, all you surrounding nations, and gather yourselves there. Bring down your warriors, O LORD. Let the nations stir themselves up and come up to the Valley of Jehoshaphat; for there I will sit to judge all the surrounding nations. Put in the sickle, for the harvest is ripe. Go in, tread, for the winepress is full. The vats overflow, for their evil is great. Multitudes, multitudes, in the valley of decision! For the day of the LORD is near in the valley of decision. The sun and the moon are darkened, and the stars withdraw their shining. The LORD roars from Zion, and utters his voice from Jerusalem, and the heavens and the earth quake. But the LORD is a refuge to his people, a stronghold to the people of Israel. "So you shall know that I am the LORD your God, who dwells in Zion, my holy mountain. And Jerusalem shall be holy, and strangers shall never again pass through it. (note: the "valley of decision" here is referring to the decision of the Lord's judgment; heathen is an old English word equivalent to nations)

Zephaniah 1:14-18 – The great day of the LORD is near, near and hastening fast; the sound of the day of the LORD is bitter; the mighty man cries aloud there. A day of wrath is that day, a day of distress and anguish, a day of ruin and devastation, a day of darkness and gloom, a day of clouds and thick darkness, a day of trumpet blast and battle cry against the fortified cities and against the lofty battlements. I will bring distress on mankind, so that they shall walk like the blind, because they have sinned against the LORD; their blood shall be poured out like dust, and their flesh like dung. Neither their silver nor their gold shall be able to deliver them on the day of the wrath of the LORD. In the fire of his jealousy, all the earth shall be consumed; for a full and sudden end he will make of all the inhabitants of the earth.

The following passage from Zechariah is a little longer than the others and contains some additional interesting details. For example, Jesus will literally, physically stand on the Mount of Olives in Jerusalem and will be King over all the earth. Not only that, there will be summer and winter, indicating that the word "day" in Day of the Lord is not a 24-hour day, but instead a longer period of time.

> **Zechariah 14:1-9** – Behold, a day is coming for the LORD, when the spoil taken from you will be divided in your midst. For I will gather all the nations against Jerusalem to battle, and the city shall be taken and the houses plundered and the women raped. Half of the city shall go out into exile, but the rest of the people shall not be cut off from the city. Then the LORD will go out and fight against those nations as when he fights on a day of battle. On that day his feet shall stand on the Mount of Olives that lies before Jerusalem on the east, and the Mount of Olives shall be split in two from east to west by a very wide valley, so that one half of the Mount shall move northward, and the other half southward. And you shall flee to the valley of my mountains, for the valley of the mountains shall reach to Azal. And you shall flee as you fled from the earthquake in the days of Uzziah king of Judah. Then the LORD my God will come, and all the holy ones with him. On that day there shall be no light, cold, or frost. And there shall be a unique day, which is known to the LORD, neither day nor night, but at evening time there shall be light. On that day living waters

shall flow out from Jerusalem, half of them to the eastern sea and half of them to the western sea. It shall continue in summer as in winter. And the LORD will be king over all the earth. On that day the LORD will be one and his name one.

More descriptions of the Day of the Lord are found in Jeremiah 46:10, Ezekiel 30:1-3, Joel 1:15, Joel 2:1-2, Amos 5:18-20, and Malachi 4:1-6. After reading these many verses above, what impression do you have of the Day of the Lord? Using the language of Scripture, it is a day of clouds and thick darkness in which the sun, moon, and stars are darkened. It is a day when the Lord executes judgment and vengeance in anger and fierce wrath and yet during it all there will be those who will be saved - "everyone who calls on the name of the LORD shall be saved" (Joel 2:32). And while Malachi 4:1 says the all the arrogant and evildoers will burn in that day, those that fear the Lord will receive healing and "shall go out leaping like calves from the stall."

Zechariah 14 shows the global scope of the Day of the Lord. Global government in and of itself is not an evil thing, but the only scenario in which a global government is going to be good is when King Jesus is ruling over it. The later verses of Zechariah 14 indicate that the Day of the Lord is more than simply a 24-hour day because "everyone who survives of all the nations that have come against Jerusalem shall go up year after year to worship the King, the LORD of hosts, and to keep the Feast of Booths" and those who fail to do so will not receive any rain, but instead will receive a plague from the Lord (Zech. 14:16-19).

New Testament Characterizations

The New Testament provides more detail about the Day of the Lord, including from the perspective of the believer. The name of the Day of the Lord is modified in some verses to "the day of our Lord Jesus Christ" (1 Cor. 1:8), "the day of our Lord Jesus" (2 Cor. 1:14), "the day of Jesus Christ" (Phil. 1:6), "the day of Christ" (Phil. 1:10, Phil. 2:16), and "the day of God" (2 Pet. 3:12). Many of these New Testament verses portray this day as a time that believers in Jesus Christ are waiting for and looking forward to rather than a time of God's vengeance and judgment. The difference is Jesus. For those who do not believe in Him, it will be a day of wrath, but for those who are in Christ it will be a day to rejoice. It is a transitional event that marks the end of one age and the beginning of another. Let's look at some of these in their immediate contexts.

> **1 Corinthians 1:6-8** – Even as the testimony about Christ was confirmed among you — so that you are not lacking in any gift, as you wait for the revealing of our Lord Jesus Christ, who will sustain you to the end, guiltless in the day of our Lord Jesus Christ.

Notice how the Day of the Lord coincides with the coming of the Lord. Also, if we are "guiltless" there is no reason to fear the wrath or judgment of the Lord in that day. Being guiltless here does not mean that Christians are living a perfectly sinless life, but that God imputes the righteousness of Christ to us and therefore sees us as righteous (Rom. 3:22, 1 Cor. 1:30, Phil. 3:9). Moreover, this verse and the verses that follow confirm that Jesus is YWHW, the LORD[14] mentioned in all the Old Testament verses about the Day of the Lord stated previously.

> **1 Corinthians 5:5** – You are to deliver this man to Satan for the destruction of the flesh, so that his spirit may be saved in the day of the Lord.

> **Philippians 1:6,10** – And I am sure of this, that he who began a good work in you will bring it to completion at the day of Jesus Christ. ... so that you may approve what is excellent, and so be pure and blameless for the day of Christ.

While there are signs that will occur before the Day of the Lord, it is also described as coming suddenly, like a thief in the night.

> **1 Thessalonians 5:1-3** – Now concerning the times and the seasons, brothers, you have no need to have anything written to you. For you yourselves are fully aware that the day of the Lord will come like a thief in the night. While people are saying, "There is peace and security," then sudden destruction will come upon them as labor pains come upon a pregnant woman, and they will not escape.

> **2 Thessalonians 2:1-4** – Now concerning the coming of our Lord Jesus Christ and our being gathered together to him, we ask you, brothers, not to be quickly shaken in mind or alarmed, either by a spirit or a spoken word, or a letter seeming to be from us, to the effect that the day of the Lord has come. Let no one deceive you in

---

14 The word LORD in all capital letters in the Old Testament is the English rendering of YWHW.

any way. For that day will not come, unless the rebellion comes first, and the man of lawlessness is revealed, the son of destruction, who opposes and exalts himself against every so-called god or object of worship, so that he takes his seat in the temple of God, proclaiming himself to be God.

This passage also reveals that one of the things that must take place before the Day of the Lord is that there will be a falling away and the man of lawlessness (*i.e.* the antichrist) will be revealed and will also enter a temple in Jerusalem and proclaim himself to be God.

2 Peter 3:10-12 – But the day of the Lord will come like a thief, and then the heavens will pass away with a roar, and the heavenly bodies will be burned up and dissolved, and the earth and the works that are done on it will be exposed. Since all these things are thus to be dissolved, what sort of people ought you to be in lives of holiness and godliness, waiting for and hastening the coming of the day of God, because of which the heavens will be set on fire and dissolved, and the heavenly bodies will melt as they burn!

The apostle Peter in the passage above shows that the "day of the Lord" can also be called the "day of God" and that it includes the heavens and the earth being burned up, which will make way for the new heaven and the new earth (Rev. 21:1). The following verse calls it the "day of God Almighty."

Revelation 16:13-14 – And I saw three unclean spirits like frogs come out of the mouth of the dragon, and out of the mouth of the beast, and out of the mouth of the false prophet. For they are the spirits of devils, working miracles, which go forth unto the kings of the earth and of the whole world, to gather them to the battle of that great day of God Almighty.

The passages that we have just looked at are not the only ones that address the events of the Day of the Lord in the New Testament. For example, when Jesus answered the disciples' question about His coming and the end of the age, He places it immediately after the great Tribulation (the second half of the 70th week of Daniel's prophecy) and cites a key sign of the Day of the Lord from Isaiah 13:10. Here is how it is stated in Mark 13:24-27:

But in those days, after that Tribulation, the sun shall be darkened, and the moon shall not give her light, And the stars of heaven shall fall, and the powers that are in heaven shall be shaken. And then shall they see the Son of man coming in the clouds with great power and glory. And then shall he send his angels, and shall gather together his elect from the four winds, from the uttermost part of the earth to the uttermost part of heaven.

The parallel passage in Matthew 24:29 says it is "immediately" after the tribulation of those days. The concept of the Lord gathering His people is seen at this event as well. Recall that the pattern found in the Old Testament was that God's blessings follow when God gathers His people. While the Day of the Lord will be a time of great judgment for the unbeliever, it will be a time of great blessing for those who believe in Christ.

Description in Revelation

The book of Revelation provides details of the Day of the Lord in four distinct prophetic passages:

1. The sixth seal (Rev. 6:12-17)

2. The seventh trumpet (Rev. 10:7, 11:15-19)

3. The seventh bowl (Rev. 16:16-21)

4. The return of Jesus Christ to earth (Rev. 19:11-21)

The events articulated in these passages not only align with each other, but they also share key characteristics with the Old Testament verses describing the Day of the Lord. For example, Isaiah 2:19 describes the men of the earth hiding in the "caves of the rocks and the holes of the ground, from before the terror of the LORD, and from the splendor of his majesty, when he rises to terrify the earth" and Isaiah 13:9-10 associates the Day of the Lord with the sun, moon, and stars being darkened. The sixth seal characterizes the sun as becoming black as sackcloth of hair, the moon becoming as blood, the stars falling to earth (Rev. 6:12-13). Moreover, the sixth seal parallels Isaiah 2:19 as it says in Revelation 6:15-17:

> Then the kings of the earth and the great ones and the generals and the rich and the powerful, and everyone, slave and free, hid themselves in the caves and among the rocks of the mountains, calling to the mountains and rocks, "Fall on us and hide us from the face of him who is seated on the throne, and from the wrath of the Lamb, for the great day of their wrath has come, and who can stand?"

The seventh trumpet declares that the mystery of God will be fulfilled (Rev. 10:7) and the kingdoms of the world will become the kingdoms of Christ and he will reign forever (Rev. 11:15). The seventh bowl includes a voice from the temple and throne in heaven saying, "It is done!" (Rev. 16:17). The sixth seal, seventh trumpet, and seventh bowl all mention an earthquake (Rev. 6:12, Rev. 11:19, Rev. 16:18). This in and of itself is not enough to conclude that these are prophesying a comment event, but it adds one more indicator to be taken with the other commonalities. The seventh trumpet and seventh bowl both say that there will be great voices out of heaven, and voices, lightning, and thunder, as well as great hail (Rev. 11:15,19, Rev: 16:18, 21). Finally, another link between the sixth seal and the seventh bowl is that both contain descriptions of mountains and islands being moved out of their places (Rev. 6:14, Rev. 16:20).

Another view of the Second Coming of Christ, which is how the Day of the Lord begins, is given in the Olivet Discourse and is harmonized in Table 1.

Table 1. *Second Coming Harmony in the Olivet Discourse.*

Matthew 24:29-31	Mark 13:24-27	Luke 21:25-28
[29] Immediately after the tribulation of those days the sun will be darkened, and the moon will not give its light, and the stars will fall from heaven, and the powers of the heavens will be shaken.	[24] But in those days, after that tribulation, the sun will be darkened, and the moon will not give its light,	[25] And there will be signs in sun and moon and stars, and on the earth distress of nations in perplexity because of the roaring of the sea and the waves,

Matthew 24:29-31	Mark 13:24-27	Luke 21:25-28
[30] And there will be signs in sun and moon and stars, and on the earth distress of nations in perplexity because of the roaring of the sea and the waves,	[25] and the stars will be falling from heaven, and the powers in the heavens will be shaken.	[26] people fainting with fear and with foreboding of what is coming on the world. For the powers of the heavens will be shaken.
[31] And he will send out his angels with a loud trumpet call, and they will gather his elect from the four winds, from one end of heaven to the other.	[26] And then they will see the Son of Man coming in clouds with great power and glory. .	[27] And then they will see the Son of Man coming in a cloud with power and great glory.
	[27] And then he will send out the angels and gather his elect from the four winds, from the ends of the earth to the ends of heaven.	[28] Now when these things begin to take place, straighten up and raise your heads, because your redemption is drawing near.

As we make the connection between the Day of the Lord and the Second Coming of Christ, Revelation 19:11-21 gives some of the most important details of how the Day of the Lord begins:

> Then I saw heaven opened, and behold, a white horse! The one sitting on it is called Faithful and True, and in righteousness he judges and makes war. His eyes are like a flame of fire, and on his head are many diadems, and he has a name written that no one knows but himself. He is clothed in a robe dipped in blood, and the name by which he is called is The Word of God. And the

armies of heaven, arrayed in fine linen, white and pure, were following him on white horses. From his mouth comes a sharp sword with which to strike down the nations, and he will rule them with a rod of iron. He will tread the winepress of the fury of the wrath of God the Almighty. On his robe and on his thigh he has a name written, King of kings and Lord of lords. Then I saw an angel standing in the sun, and with a loud voice he called to all the birds that fly directly overhead, "Come, gather for the great supper of God, to eat the flesh of kings, the flesh of captains, the flesh of mighty men, the flesh of horses and their riders, and the flesh of all men, both free and slave, both small and great." And I saw the beast and the kings of the earth with their armies gathered to make war against him who was sitting on the horse and against his army. And the beast was captured, and with it the false prophet who in its presence had done the signs by which he deceived those who had received the mark of the beast and those who worshiped its image. These two were thrown alive into the lake of fire that burns with sulfur. And the rest were slain by the sword that came from the mouth of him who was sitting on the horse, and all the birds were gorged with their flesh.

Who is the one on the white horse whose name is called the Word of God? If you have any doubt that this is Jesus the Messiah, then consult John 1:1-4 and John 1:14. All of the other descriptions of this person clearly identify Him as Jesus as well. Notice that His purpose here is to judge and make war in righteousness (Rev. 19:11). While His name is the Word of God and Jesus Himself is the Word (Jn. 1:1), the sword that proceeds from His mouth must be the written word of God (Heb. 4:12, Rev. 1:16).

By His word He will strike down the nations (Rev. 19:15). Hosea 6:5 says that God can slay by the words of His mouth. Look at some of the other verses from the Bible that describe the power and effects of God's word in judging the wicked.

> **Isaiah 11:4** – But with righteousness he shall judge the poor, and decide with equity for the meek of the earth; and he shall strike the earth with the rod of his mouth, and with the breath of his lips he shall kill the wicked.

> **Isaiah 49:2** – He made my mouth like a sharp sword; in the shadow of his hand he hid me; he made me a polished arrow; in his quiver he hid me away.

> **Isaiah 66:15-16** – For behold, the LORD will come in fire, and his chariots like the whirlwind, to render his anger in fury, and his rebuke with flames of fire. For by fire will the LORD enter into judgment, and by his sword, with all flesh; and those slain by the LORD shall be many.

> **Zephaniah 1:18** – Neither their silver nor their gold shall be able to deliver them on the day of the wrath of the LORD. In the fire of his jealousy, all the earth shall be consumed; for a full and sudden end he will make of all the inhabitants of the earth.

2 Thessalonians 1:7-10 – And to grant relief to you who are afflicted as well as to us, when the Lord Jesus is revealed from heaven with his mighty angels in flaming fire, inflicting vengeance on those who do not know God and on those who do not obey the gospel of our Lord Jesus. They will suffer the punishment of eternal destruction, away from the presence of the Lord and from the glory of his might, when he comes on that day to be glorified in his saints, and to be marveled at among all who have believed, because our testimony to you was believed.

The previous passage from 2 Thessalonians shows the contrast in the outcomes in the Day of the Lord depending on one's response to the gospel. To *obey* the gospel means to *believe* it (Rom. 16:26, Heb. 5:9, 1 Pet. 1:2). Do you know the gospel? Do you believe it?

The return of the Lord Jesus to earth is an event that everyone will see (Isa. 40:5, Isa. 52:10, Isa. 66:18). God's voice will shake not only earth but heaven also (Heb. 12:26-28, Isa. 2:19, 21, Isa. 13:13, Joel 3:16, Hag. 2:6-7).

Judgment of the Antichrist and False Prophet

Though all of His saints and angels will return with Jesus, He is the one who will be executing justice and judgment when He comes. This will begin with the two head honchos of the Tribulation. The antichrist (beast) and false prophet will be "thrown alive into the lake of fire that burns with sulfur" (Rev. 19:20). The lake of fire is the place of final judgment in the Bible. In Daniel 11:29-45, the exploits of the antichrist are prophesied as well as his demise, which is simply described as, "Yet he shall come to his end, with none to help him."

Judgment of the Kings and Armies Aligned with the Antichrist

A day is coming when all the nations of the earth and their leaders will gather their military forces around Jerusalem (Zech. 12:1-3, Zech. 14:1-3, Rev. 16:13-16, Rev. 19:19). After Jesus throws the antichrist and false prophet into the lake of fire, he will kill the remaining armies coming against Jerusalem by His words, which is the sword of His mouth, the word of God (Rev. 19:20-21).

Judgment of the Remaining People on Earth at that Time

After throwing the beast and false prophet into the lake of fire and destroying the military forces aligned against Him, Jesus will turn His attention to the remaining people alive on the earth at that time. They will be gathered and separated into two groups: believers and unbelievers, just as a shepherd divides sheep and goats (Mt. 25:31-46). The believers will be welcomed into the kingdom while the unbelievers will be killed and their souls to be held in Hades to eventually to be thrown into the lake of fire for everlasting punishment at the judgment that will occur after the Millennial Kingdom at the great white throne (Rev. 20:11-15).

In the Old Testament, this separation is prophesied in Isaiah 66:15-16, Jeremiah 25:31-33, and Joel 3:2-14. These passages speak of the Lord gathering all the nations and entering into judgment against all people, with the wicked being given to the sword. The only way not to be seen as wicked by God is to be in Christ by faith (Phil. 3:9). In the New Testament, the parable told by Jesus in Matthew 25:31-46 describes this as a separation of sheep and goats, with their faith evidenced by their works, particularly toward His brethren, the Jews. To the sheep, He says, "Come, you who are blessed by my Father, inherit the kingdom prepared for you from the foundation of the world" and of the goats, "these will go away into eternal punishment" (Mt. 25:34,46). In Matthew 24:37-41, part of the Olivet Discourse, the return of Christ is likened to the days of Noah. The parallel is that in the same way the flood removed everyone on earth who was not in the ark, Jesus will remove everyone on earth who is not in Him by faith.

Ezekiel 20:33-38 is a prophetic passage that describes how God will gather Israel from all the countries of the world where they had been scattered and will enter into judgment with them face to face. Here is that passage:

> As I live, declares the Lord GOD, surely with a mighty hand and an outstretched arm and with

> wrath poured out I will be king over you. I will bring you out from the peoples and gather you out of the countries where you are scattered, with a mighty hand and an outstretched arm, and with wrath poured out. And I will bring you into the wilderness of the peoples, and there I will enter into judgment with you face to face. As I entered into judgment with your fathers in the wilderness of the land of Egypt, so I will enter into judgment with you, declares the Lord GOD. I will make you pass under the rod, and I will bring you into the bond of the covenant. I will purge out the rebels from among you, and those who transgress against me. I will bring them out of the land where they sojourn, but they shall not enter the land of Israel. Then you will know that I am the LORD.

God will bring the Jews into a wilderness area during the second half of the Tribulation period (Rev. 12:6) and when He returns He will "plead" with them in the sense that He will judge each person. To "pass under the rod" is how a shepherd would evaluate his sheep. To bring them into the "bond of the covenant" will be to see who among them are in the new covenant by faith in Jesus the Messiah. Those that are not in faith will be purged out and not be permitted to enter the land of Israel. Those that have faith in Jesus will experience what is prophesied in Jeremiah 32:37-41:

> Behold, I will gather them from all the countries to which I drove them in my anger and my wrath and in great indignation. I will bring them back to this place, and I will make them dwell in safety. And they shall be my people, and I will be their

God. I will give them one heart and one way, that they may fear me forever, for their own good and the good of their children after them. I will make with them an everlasting covenant, that I will not turn away from doing good to them. And I will put the fear of me in their hearts, that they may not turn from me. I will rejoice in doing them good, and I will plant them in this land in faithfulness, with all my heart and all my soul.

In the same way that God became known as the Lord who "brought up the people of Israel out of the land of Egypt," in the future He will become known as the God who "led the offspring of the house of Israel out of the north country, and out of all the countries where he had driven them; and that they then dwell in their own land" (Jer. 23:3-8).

This judging of Jews and Gentiles might be what occupies the additional 30 (1290 - 1260 = 30) and 75 days (1335 - 1260 = 75) beyond the midpoint of the Tribulation spoken of in Daniel 12:11-12. The temple described in Ezekiel 40-48 could possibly be built and purified during this time.

Judgment of Satan

Revelation 20:1-3 succinctly describes what will happen to Satan when Jesus returns to the earth.

Then I saw an angel coming down from heaven, holding in his hand the key to the bottomless pit and a great chain. And he seized the dragon, that ancient serpent, who is the devil and Satan, and

> bound him for a thousand years, and threw him into the pit, and shut it and sealed it over him, so that he might not deceive the nations any longer, until the thousand years were ended. After that he must be released for a little while.

We'll look at what will happen during the thousand years that Satan is bound in the bottomless pit as well as what will happen when he is released when we discuss the Millennial Kingdom.

Like a Thief in the Night

The timing of the Day of the Lord is compared to a "thief in the night" (1 Thes. 5:2, 2 Pet. 3:10). The implication in that phrase is that it will be a shocking surprise, and not in a good way. But for whom will the Day of the Lord be like a thief in the night? The Bible indicates that the Day of the Lord will not come upon everyone in this way, but only those that are "in darkness" and "of the night." (1 Thes. 5:2-5). In these verses, Paul makes a clear distinction between believers ("we" and "you") and unbelievers ("they" and "them") and that the Day of the Lord will *not* overtake the believers like a thief. As for the unbelievers, 1 Thessalonians 5:3 states it this way:

> While people are saying, "There is peace and security," then sudden destruction will come upon them as labor pains come upon a pregnant woman, and they will not escape.

Jesus warns the world to watch for His return in several parables in the Olivet Discourse and to "stay awake" (Mt. 24:42 - 25:30, Mk. 13:35-37), but His warnings are unheeded by those who don't believe in Him. People who don't believe the Bible will not heed its warnings or obey its commands. This is one of the reasons Jesus compares the days preceding His return to the days of Noah (Mt. 24:37-41). Even though Noah built the ark and preached publicly about the impending flood for a dozen decades, no one joined his family in entering the ark, even after seeing pairs of animals miraculously entering it. Instead, they continued with life as usual, eating, drinking, marrying, working in their fields, and grinding at their mills until the flood came and took their lives.

Two verses from the book of Revelation also show the connection between repentance/salvation and Jesus surprising them like a thief when He returns:

Revelation 3:3 – Remember, then, what you received and heard. Keep it, and repent. If you will not wake up, I will come like a thief, and you will not know at what hour I will come against you.

Revelation 16:15 – Behold, I am coming like a thief! Blessed is the one who stays awake, keeping his garments on, that he may not go about naked and be seen exposed!

If they choose to, and if they believe it, people living in the Tribulation period will be able to read the signs and determine the timing of the Day of the Lord and not be surprised by it. If they observe when a seven-year covenant is confirmed with Israel, they could know that the Day of the Lord will be exactly seven years from that day. When they see the antichrist proclaim himself to be God in the Temple, they could look ahead 1260 days to know when the Day of the Lord will begin [15]. However, those who don't trust God through Jesus don't believe the Bible and pay no attention to His word, so this event will catch them by surprise, like a thief in the night.

Who is Returning with Him?

Looking again into Revelation 19, verse 14 mentions armies coming with Him from heaven also on white horses and wearing clean, fine, white linen. Who can this be? In Revelation 19:7-8 the wife of the Lamb is clothed in clean, fine, white linen. When Jesus returns, He will bring with Him all His saints according to the following verses.

Zechariah 14:5 – – And you shall flee to the valley of my mountains, for the valley of the mountains shall reach to Azal. And you shall flee as you fled from the earthquake in the days of Uzziah king of Judah. Then the LORD my God will come, *and all the holy ones with him. (emphasis mine)*

1 Thessalonians 3:13 – So that he may establish your hearts blameless in holiness before our God and Father, at the coming of our Lord Jesus *with all his saints. (emphasis mine)*

Also see Matthew 24:30-31, Mark 13:26-27, 1 Thessalonians 2:19, and 4:14. In the Bible, saints are holy ones, and the name saint, which literally

---

15 More will be said about this topic in the subsection *When is the Rapture* in the section called *The Rapture* of this book.

means holy one or one who is set apart, is a way of identifying all people who have ever trusted in Jesus Christ throughout all of time.

All of those who have been raptured prior to the Lord's return will have received their glorified bodies (1 Cor. 15:50-57). Look at this description given in Isaiah 62:11-12:

> Behold, the LORD has proclaimed to the end of the earth: Say to the daughter of Zion, "Behold, your salvation comes; behold, his reward is with him, and his recompense before him." And they shall be called The Holy People, The Redeemed of the LORD; and you shall be called Sought Out, A City Not Forsaken.

Who is the "they" that will be called, "The Holy People, The Redeemed of the LORD?" Could it be those saints with glorified bodies that return with Him? In Revelation 22:12 Jesus says, "Behold, I am coming soon, bringing my recompense with me, to repay each one for what he has done," and Isaiah 35:9-10 says about this time that "the redeemed shall walk there" and "the ransomed of the LORD shall return and come to Zion with singing; everlasting joy shall be upon their heads; they shall obtain gladness and joy, and sorrow and sighing shall flee away."

When Jesus returns to the earth at His Second Coming, He will not only bring all His saints, but will also be accompanied by all the holy angels, who are also referred to as "his angels" (Mt. 16:27, Mt. 25:31, Mk. 8:38, Lk. 9:26).

114

The Millennial (Messianic) Kingdom and Beyond

The Day of the Lord will continue for a thousand years from the time that Jesus returns in person and Satan is bound in the bottomless pit and then for "a little while" after Satan is released from the pit (Rev. 20:1-3). This thousand-year period is commonly referred to by Christians as the Millennial Kingdom. The Messianic Kingdom would also be an appropriate name for it since Jesus the Messiah will be ruling over it. In the model prayer that Jesus taught, recorded in Matthew 6:9-10, we read this:

> Pray then like this: "Our Father in heaven, hallowed be your name. *Your kingdom come,* your will be done, on earth as it is in heaven." *(emphasis mine)*

This is the kingdom that is coming, and Jesus will be King over it in all the earth (Zech. 14:9). Jesus is the King of the kingdom that is represented by the stone that was "cut out by no human hand" that becomes a mountain and fills the whole earth, consumes all the previous nations, and stands forever (Dan. 2:34-35, 44-45).

Some people say the kingdom is here now. This is not correct. Christians on earth now are currently *ambassadors* (2 Cor. 5:20), meaning that we are representing our home country (heaven) while we are residing in a foreign country (earth). However, as believers in Christ, we are currently citizens of the kingdom by virtue of our standing in Christ and even seated in heavenly places with Him because we are in Him (Col. 1:13, Eph. 2:6, Phil. 3:20). Every time someone on earth places saving faith in Jesus Christ, the kingdom gains a new citizen.

Details of this kingdom are found in many different places in the Bible, particularly in the Old Testament whenever God mentions when He will *gather* Israel. Many important features are revealed in the New Testament as well. Let's take a look at the characteristics of this coming kingdom.

Ruling with a Rod of Iron

We read previously in Revelation 19:15 that when Jesus returns He will rule the nations with a rod of iron. Psalm 2:6 and Revelation 12:5 also say this. At first glance, this may seem very harsh, and it will be for those who oppose Him. But digging into the underlying Greek that these words are translated from also reveals a gracious side to this phrase. Using a concordance to examine how the Holy Spirit uses these words in Scripture, we see the following.

- rule (Gr: *poimainō*) = rule (4x, as in Mt. 2:6) or feed (6x, as in Jn. 21:16, Acts 20:28, 1 Pet. 5:2, Rev. 7:17) or feed cattle (1x); note that *poimēn* means shepherd

- rod (Gr: *rhabdos*) = rod (6x, as in 1 Cor. 4:21 or Heb. 9:4), staff (4x, as in Mk. 6:8), scepter (2x, as in Heb. 1:8)

116

- iron (Gr: *sidērous*) = iron (5x); see Dan. 2:40 to see that iron symbolizes something strong

Does this change your impression of what it means to rule with a rod of iron? Think of a shepherd feeding his sheep and conveying strength in the way he uses his staff or a king generously teaching his subjects while ruling over them with a strong scepter. Loving, yet firm, dealing swiftly and strongly with sin. When Jesus is ruling the world with a rod of iron in the coming kingdom, people from all over the world will come to Jerusalem saying, "Come, let us go up to the mountain of the LORD, to the house of the God of Jacob, that he may teach us his ways and that we may walk in his paths" (Isa. 2:2-3, Mic. 4:1-2). Not only that, Jesus will "judge between the nations, and shall decide disputes for many peoples" (Isa. 2:4, Mic. 4:3). Keep reading and you will see abundant goodness, prosperity, and peace in this kingdom.

Two Thrones

During the thousand-year reign we call the Millennial Kingdom, Jesus will reign over all the earth as King. But isn't Jesus currently occupying a throne? The answer is "Yes!" but we must understand that there is more than one throne in the Bible. Consider Revelation 3:21:

> The one who conquers, I will grant him to sit with me on *my* throne, as I also conquered and sat down with my Father on *his* throne. *(emphasis mine)*

Notice in this verse that Jesus has a throne, and the Father also has a throne. The Father's throne is in heaven (Ps. 11:4, Rev. 4:2, Rev. 5:1-7). But what is the throne Jesus is referring to as "my throne" in Revelation 3:21? In the angel Gabriel's prophetic words to Mary, he says:

> **Luke 1:31-32** – And behold, you will conceive in your womb and bear a son, and you shall call his name Jesus. He will be great and will be called the Son of the Most High. And the Lord God will give to him the throne of his father David.

It just doesn't make sense to say that the "throne of his father David" is a reference to God's throne in heaven. It must certainly be talking about the throne of the nation of Israel in Jerusalem.

Jesus refers to this throne as "his glorious throne" and places it chronologically after He returns to earth:

> **Matthew 25:31-32** –*When the Son of Man comes in his glory, and all the angels with him, then he will sit on his glorious throne.* Before him will be gathered all the nations, and he will separate people one from another as a shepherd separates the sheep from the goats. *(emphasis mine)*

> **Matthew 19:28-29** – Jesus said to them, "Truly, I say to you, *in the new world, when the Son of Man will sit on his glorious throne,* you who have followed me will also sit on twelve thrones, judging the twelve tribes of Israel. And everyone who has left houses or brothers or sisters or father or mother or children or lands, for my name's sake, will receive a hundredfold and will inherit eternal life." *(emphasis mine)*

Jesus coming to the earth in His glory is the dividing point between the current age and the age to come.

Here are more verses on this topic that verify that even though He currently sits on the throne in heaven with God the Father, Jesus will eventually occupy the throne of David on earth.

> **Acts 2:29-31** – Brothers, I may say to you with confidence about the patriarch David that he both died and was buried, and his tomb is with us to this day. Being therefore a prophet, and knowing that *God had sworn with an oath to him that he would set one of his descendants on his throne,* he foresaw and spoke about the resurrection of the Christ, that he was not abandoned to Hades, nor did his flesh see corruption. *(emphasis mine)*

> **Isaiah 9:6-7** – For to us a child is born, to us a son is given; and the government shall be upon his shoulder, and his name shall be called Wonderful Counselor, Mighty God, Everlasting Father, Prince of Peace. Of the increase of his government and of peace there will be no end, *on the throne of David and over his kingdom,* to establish it and to uphold it with justice and with righteousness from this time forth and forevermore. The zeal of the LORD of hosts will do this. *(emphasis mine)*

> **Isaiah 16:5** – Then a throne will be established in steadfast love, and on it will sit in faithfulness in the tent of David one who judges and seeks justice and is swift to do righteousness.

> **1 Kings 2:45** – But King Solomon shall be blessed, and the throne of David shall be established before the LORD forever.

Psalm 132:11 – The LORD swore to David a sure oath from which he will not turn back: "One of the sons of your body I will set on your throne."

There is no doubt that Jesus is currently ruling over all of the universe as its Creator and Sustainer (Col. 1:16-17). He is just not yet sitting on David's throne in Jerusalem.

The Saints Who Return with Jesus

The Bible provides clear insight into the big-picture view of what those who return with Him will do during this Millennial Kingdom time period. Consider these verses:

Revelation 2:26-27 – The one who conquers and who keeps my works until the end, to him I will give authority over the nations, and he will rule them with a rod of iron, as when earthen pots are broken in pieces, even as I myself have received authority from my Father.

Revelation 20:4-6 – Then I saw thrones, and seated on them were those to whom the authority to judge was committed. Also I saw the souls of those who had been beheaded for the testimony of Jesus and for the word of God, and those who had not worshiped the beast or its image and had not received its mark on their foreheads or their hands. *They came to life and reigned with Christ for a thousand years.* The rest of the dead did not come to life until the thousand years were ended. This is the first resurrection. Blessed and holy is the one who shares in the first resurrection! Over such the second death has no power, but *they will be priests of God and of Christ, and they will reign with him for a thousand years. (emphasis mine)*

Matthew 19:27-29 – Then Peter said in reply, "See, we have left everything and followed you. What then will we have?" Jesus said to them, "Truly, I say to you, *in the new world, when the Son of Man will sit on his glorious throne, you who have followed me will also sit on twelve thrones, judging the twelve tribes of Israel.* And everyone who has left houses or brothers or sisters or father or mother or children or lands, for my name's sake, will receive a hundredfold and will inherit eternal life. *(emphasis mine)*

1 Corinthians 6:2-3 – Or do you not know that *the saints will judge the world*? And if the world is to be judged by you, are you incompetent to try trivial cases? 3 Do you not know that *we are to judge angels?* How much more, then, matters pertaining to this life! *(emphasis mine)*

We will rule under Jesus as priests reigning in the kingdom of God on the earth (Rev. 5:6-10, Rev. 20:6). We, too, will rule with a rod of iron with the authority given by His throne. Remember that ruling with an iron rod is another way of saying to feed with a strong staff or scepter and having no tolerance for sin. If you are wondering what it means to be one that overcomes as in Revelation 2:26, first John 5:5 explains that one who believes Jesus is the Son of God is one that overcomes the world.

What does it mean when Paul says that we will "judge the world?" In the Bible, the idea of judging can be one of using biblical wisdom to settle disputes, give wise counsel, justify the righteous, and condemn the wicked (Ex. 18:15-27, Deut. 16:18-20, Deut. 25:1, Jdg. 4:5, 1 Kings 3:16-28, Lk. 7:41-43). The example in 1 Kings 3:16-28 of Solomon settling the dispute between the two prostitute women where one was the mother of the living baby, and one was the mother of the baby who died is very instructive about this concept. The incident ends with this statement in 1 Kings 3:28:

> And all Israel heard of the *judgment* that the king had rendered, and they stood in awe of the king, because they perceived that the wisdom of God was in him to do *justice. (emphasis mine)*

Since the saints who return with the Lord will already have glorified bodies (1 Cor. 15:51-53), won't it be weird to have a mix of glorified bodies and unglorified bodies at the same time? Not really. It's been done before. Recall that Jesus walked among His disciples for 40 days after His resurrection and glorification, even appearing before 500 of His followers at once (Acts. 1:3, 1 Cor. 15:6). He ate food with His disciples and explained to them that He was "flesh and bones," even inviting Thomas to touch His hands and side (Lk. 24:36-43, Jn. 20:24-28, Jn. 21:12-14).

Gathering of Israel – Promises Fulfilled

As discussed previously, when the Bible speaks of God gathering Israel, the descriptions are of great blessings. When Israel is gathered one last time, after being scattered for the last time, all the promises of these blessings will come to pass. This will be such a gathering of Israel that God will be characterized by it in the same way that He became known as the God "who brought up the people of Israel out of the land of Egypt," only this will be on a much grander scale (Jer. 16:14-15, Jer. 25:31-34).

In Genesis 12:7, 13:14-17, and 15:18 God promises Abraham and his "offspring" that He will give them the land that He showed to him. And while Galatians 3:16 states that in one of these passages the offspring of Abraham in God's promise was the singular version of offspring and refers to Christ, it is also clear from these and many others that the descendants of Abraham, Isaac, and Jacob are in mind here.

Consider the question and answer recorded in Acts 1:1-8. We are told how Jesus taught His apostles (Jews who knew the Old Testament very well) about "the kingdom of God" during the 40 days after His resurrection and the only question they asked recorded in Scripture is "Lord, will you at this time restore the kingdom to Israel?" Note that His answer wasn't, *"You don't understand, all of that was allegory and figurative language"* but was, "It is not for you to know times or seasons that the Father has fixed by his own authority."

A defining feature of the Jubilee is that the tribes of Israel will be returned to their original lands (Lev. 25:10, 13). In the Scripture passages about God's promises to gather Israel, they specifically describe the location of the gathering as the land of their fathers/ancestors (Deut. 30:5, Jer. 16:15, Jer. 30:3, Ez. 36:11). Ezekiel 47:13-21 is very specific about the borders of this land. Jesus tells his disciples that they will sit on 12 thrones and rule over the 12 tribes of Israel in His kingdom (Mt. 19:27-28, Lk. 22:29-30).

Rather than being viewed as a horror, a curse, and a byword among the nations of the world as they currently are now, which is a judgment from God, (Deut. 28:37, 1 Ki. 9:7, Jer. 24:9, Jer. 29:18, Jer. 44:22), Jerusalem and Jews will be seen around the world as a praise and a blessing (Isa. 62:7, Zeph. 3:19-20, Zech. 8:13). In God's own words from the prophet Jeremiah (Jer. 23:3-6):

> Then I will gather the remnant of my flock out of all the countries where I have driven them, and I will bring them back to their fold, and they shall be fruitful and multiply. I will set shepherds over them who will care for them, and they shall fear no more, nor be dismayed, neither shall any be missing, declares the LORD. Behold, the days are coming, declares the LORD, when I will raise up for David a righteous Branch, and he shall reign as king and deal wisely, and shall execute justice and righteousness in the land. In his days Judah will be saved, and Israel will dwell securely. And this is the name by which he will be called: "The LORD is our righteousness."

People from around the world come to Jerusalem to pray and seek the Lord and to be taught by God and to walk in His ways (Isa. 2:2-3, Zech. 8:21-23, Mic. 4:1-2). Zechariah 8:23 says this about that those days:

> Thus says the LORD of hosts: In those days ten men from the nations of every tongue shall take hold of the robe of a Jew, saying, "Let us go with you, for we have heard that God is with you."

Moreover, the Bible says that David, yes, *that* king David, will be in this kingdom shepherding the people as a prince among them ((Jer. 30:4-9, Ez. 34:23-34, Ez. 37:24-25, Ez. 46:10-18). If you are like the Bereans of Acts 17:10-11 and study the Bible to verify this claim in the verses cited here, take note that the context of each is when God gathers Israel from the nations.

Life in the Kingdom

For Jews who come to true faith in Jesus during the Tribulation and enter the kingdom at His return, the kingdom will begin with a period of mourning. The Bible describes that when they see Jesus, the one whom they pierced, they will mourn and weep bitterly as one who grieves for a firstborn son who has died (Zech. 12:8-14, Mt. 24:30, Rev. 1:7). To those who mourn, the Lord prophetically promises in Isaiah 61:2-3:

> To proclaim the year of the LORD's favor, and the day of vengeance of our God; to comfort all who mourn; to grant to those who mourn in Zion — to give them a beautiful headdress instead of ashes, the oil of gladness instead of mourning, the garment of praise instead of a faint spirit; that

they may be called oaks of righteousness, the planting of the LORD, that he may be glorified.

Recall our prior discussion of Luke 4:16-21 where we looked at how when Jesus read these verses in the synagogue that He stopped reading at "to proclaim the year of the LORD's favor." His focus was on His First Coming when He read that. The "day of vengeance" refers to His Second Coming and how God will comfort those who are mourning at that time. God will comfort and lift up those who mourn (Mt. 5:4, Jas. 4:9-10). Beyond this, there will be Eden-like conditions all over the earth, similar to what life was like before mankind's fall into sin.

There will be no more war (Isa. 2:4, Isa. 14:7, Mic. 4:3), no hunger or starvation (Deut. 30:9, Isa. 30:23-24, Ez. 36:29-30, Zech. 8:12), and no sickness or poor health because miraculous healings will accompany Jesus' appearance on earth once again (Isa. 33:24, Isa. 35:4-6, Jer. 30:17, Zech. 12:8). One must wonder if there will even be hospitals, police departments, or armies. Work will be enjoyable as it, no doubt, had to have been before the Fall since everything was good prior to that (Isa. 65:22-23). Animals will not hurt each other or people (Isa. 11:6-9, Isa. 35:9, Isa. 65:25) and will eat only plants as it was in Eden (Isa. 11:6-9, Isa. 65:25, Gen. 1:30).

The curse of Babel will be reversed because God will return the people to a "pure speech" so that people can call on Him and serve Him with one accord (Zeph. 3:9). It will be a joyful time, full of rejoicing, peace, safety, and rest (Isa. 14:7, Isa. 30:19, Isa. 35:2, Isa. 65:18-19,

Zeph. 3:14-17, Zech. 8:4-5, Zech. 14:11). In fact, God Himself will "rejoice over you with gladness; he will quiet you by his love, he will exult over you with loud singing" (Zeph. 3:17).

For those who enter this kingdom in flesh-and-blood, natural, yet-to-be glorified bodies, they will unfortunately still be subject to sin and death but will live to be hundreds of years old (Isa. 65:20-23). Isaiah prophesies that dying at 100 years old will be like a child dying and that the general lifespan will be like that of trees, which can live to be hundreds of years old (Isa. 65:20, 22). While it was after mankind's fall into sin, the Scriptures record many people of the pre-flood era who lived to be hundreds of years old (Gen. 5). Creation will continue to be "groaning" (Rom. 8:22) during this Messianic Kingdom, though that groaning will be alleviated somewhat as I have just described. The curse brought about initially by the sin of Adam in the garden of Eden will be completely removed when Jesus "delivers the kingdom to God, the Father; after destroying every rule and every authority and power" and finally "last enemy to be destroyed is death" (1 Cor. 15:24-26). We'll dive deeper into the details of this when we discuss the new heavens and the new earth.

Yet Another Temple in Jerusalem

The Bible implies that a temple will be built in Jerusalem before the midpoint of the Tribulation because the Antichrist will cause the sacrifices there to cease and declare to the world that he is God (Dan. 9:26-27, Mt. 24:15, 2 Thes. 2:3-4). Similarly, there is an inference that this new temple will be destroyed when Jesus returns on the Day of the Lord and a new temple will be built for use during the Millennial Kingdom. Zechariah 6:12-13 says:

> And say to him, "Thus says the LORD of hosts, 'Behold, the man whose name is the Branch: for he shall branch out from his place, *and he shall build the temple of the LORD. It is he who shall build the temple of the LORD* and shall bear royal honor, *and shall sit and rule on his throne.* And there shall be a priest on his throne, and the counsel of peace shall be between them both.'" *(emphasis mine)*

The Branch in these verses is Jesus (Isa. 11:1) and note that the building of this temple coincides with Him sitting and ruling on His throne. In the End Times context of Ezekiel 36-39, chapters 40 through 48 of Ezekiel describe very specific details of a temple to be built in Jerusalem.

In addition to the many physical aspects to the structure, the vision God gave Ezekiel also says that "the glory of the God of Israel" will come from the East and will enter this temple (Ez. 43:1-5). Referring to this glory of the God of Israel, Ezekiel uses masculine personal pronouns to say, "the sound of *his* coming was like the sound of many waters" and "the earth shone with *his* glory." The glory also had the same appearance that Ezekiel saw by the river Chebar, causing him to fall upon his face as he did

128

at that previous vision (Ez. 1:28, Ez. 43:3). Ezekiel is comparing the "glory of the God of Israel" in Ezekiel 43:1-5 to this magnificent vision in Ezekiel 1:26-28:

> And above the expanse over their heads there was the likeness of a throne, in appearance like sapphire; and seated above the likeness of a throne was a *likeness with a human appearance.* And upward from what had the appearance of his waist I saw as it were gleaming metal, like the appearance of fire enclosed all around. And downward from what had the appearance of his waist I saw as it were the appearance of fire, and *there was brightness around him.* Like the appearance of the bow that is in the cloud on the day of rain, so was the appearance of the brightness all around. *Such was the appearance of the likeness of the glory of the LORD.* And when I saw it, I fell on my face, and I heard the voice of one speaking. *(emphasis mine)*

Ezekiel goes on to recount in this vision that as the glory of the Lord filled the temple that a voice came out of the temple saying that "this is the place of my throne and the place of the soles of my feet, where I will dwell in the midst of the people of Israel forever," and that Israel would no longer defile His holy name or commit idolatry (Ez. 43:5-12). As I see it, this all means that Jesus himself will enter the temple that is described by Ezekiel and the Millennial Kingdom characteristics of Israel being obedient and God dwelling with them forever.

One of the aspects of Ezekiel's description of the temple in the Millennial Kingdom that may be offensive to Christians is that the Bible clearly indicates that sacrifices will be performed there (Ez. 43:19-27, Ez. 44:28-29, Ez. 45:15-25, Ez. 46:4-7). As Bible-believing Christians, we know that Jesus was the one sacrifice for all sins and that no other sacrifice is needed (Heb. 9:26, Heb. 10:12-18). Admittedly, there is a tension here and I struggle to understand this aspect of the Millennial Kingdom. If you know of a better explanation that is true to the text I'd love to hear it!

To reconcile this, think of the purpose of all the sacrifices made at the temple that were prescribed by God's word in the Old Testament period. Did they take away sins? Does the blood of bulls and goats take away sins (Heb. 10:4)? Most certainly not! Then what were they for? They were all to point to and teach about the ultimate sacrifice that Jesus Christ made at Calvary. The Old Testament sacrifices were looking forward to what Jesus would come and do on the cross. The sacrifices that will be performed in the Messianic Kingdom will be to look back and teach about the sacrifice that Jesus made in the past. Life will be so good and so peaceful in the Millennial Kingdom that people will need a reminder of the horror of sin and to teach about the sacrifice that Jesus made to provide salvation for mankind.

Before we leave the topic of the temple, let's be clear about the different temples and tabernacles revealed in the Bible. Hebrews chapters 8 and 9 show that there is a true tabernacle in heaven and a tabernacle that Israel built and used during the time of their wandering in the desert. God revealed the plan for Israel's tabernacle to Moses and it was

130

patterned after the heavenly tabernacle (Heb. 8:5). Then there was the first temple built in Jerusalem by King Solomon (1 Ki. 6) and the subsequent rebuilt temple in Jerusalem after the Jews returned from exile in Babylon (Ezra 3-6). This second temple was eventually dismantled by the Roman army in AD 70 so thoroughly that not one stone was left upon another (Mt. 24:1-2). Since the pouring out of the Holy Spirit on the day of Pentecost in AD 30, the body of Christ, which is made up of all those on earth who believe in Jesus Christ, is currently the temple of God. The next physical temple that will be built on earth will be the one that unbelieving Jews will construct and use during the first half of the tribulation period and the Antichrist will stop the sacrifices performed there and declare himself to be God. This Tribulation temple will be followed by the temple described in this section: the temple that will function during the Millennial Kingdom. The new heavens and new earth that will follow the Millennial Kingdom will not contain a temple because "its temple is the Lord God the Almighty and the Lamb" (Rev. 21:22).

One Final Rebellion at the End of the 1000 Years

While there will be centuries of great blessings during the Millennial Kingdom, it won't be perfect. People will still die (Isa. 65:20), people will still need to be rebuked by King Jesus as He decides disputes among them (Isa. 2:4, Mic, 4:3), and the families of the earth that fail to go to Jerusalem each year to worship

Jesus during the feast of tabernacles will be punished with a drought (Zech. 14:16-18). People that enter the Millennial Kingdom with natural bodies will still have children (Deut. 30:5, Isa. 65:23, Jer. 30:19, Ez. 37:25, Ez. 47:22), and although these original people that enter the kingdom will be believers, their descendants will need to place their faith in Jesus to obtain eternal life in Christ.

Satan will be confined to a "bottomless pit," also called the abyss, for the thousand-year duration of the Messianic Kingdom so that he can no longer deceive the nations (Rev. 20:1-3). However, Bible prophecy tells us that at the end of that thousand years, Satan will be released for a little season and will deceive the nations once againfor "a little while" (Rev. 20:3,7-8). Sadly, many people born during the thousaand years will not place their faith in Jesus Christ and will be swept into Satan's last deception. Revelation 20:7-9 describes the final rebellion and its conclusion very succinctly:

> And when the thousand years are ended, Satan will be released from his prison and will come out to deceive the nations that are at the four corners of the earth, Gog and Magog, to gather them for battle; their number is like the sand of the sea. And they marched up over the broad plain of the earth and surrounded the camp of the saints and the beloved city, but fire came down from heaven and consumed them.

Satan's final failed attempt to overthrow God and destroy His people leads to his eternal destiny: to be "tormented day and night forever and ever" (Rev. 20:10).

132

The Great White Throne Judgment

Following Satan's demise and the death of all those involved in that final rebellion, God will sit on a "great white throne" and administer the final judgment to all those throughout human history who have died without ever placing faith in Christ (Rev. 20:11-15). This final judgment is for "the dead" (Rev. 20:12) and, therefore, only a judgment for unbelievers, since those who believe in Christ are truly alive even if their physical bodies have died (Mk. 12:27, Jn. 11:25-26, Phil. 1:20-23). The dead, those without faith in Christ, will be judged for their works and cast into the lake of fire to be tormented for eternity (Rev. 20:13-15, Mt. 25:41-46). This punishment is called the "second death" (Rev. 20:14).

If there is a second death, then a first death is implied, but not specifically called by that title in the Bible. A reasonable inference, however, is that one's physical death, when the soul departs from the body, is the first death. Hebrews 9:27 claims that "it is appointed for man to die once, and after that comes judgment." For unbelievers, that judgment is the second death, which ultimately leads to them being cast into the lake of fire.

However, Revelation 20:6 says, "Blessed and holy is the one who shares in the first resurrection! Over such the second death has no power, but they will be priests of God and of Christ, and they will reign with him for a thousand years." The Bible does not describe the nature of the first resurrection, but

133

Revelation 20:6, implies that this refers to those who have been saved by faith in Christ. It seems reasonable to conclude that the first resurrection is a reference to believers who receive a glorified body. First Thessalonians 4:16 and 1 Corinthians 15:52 describe the Rapture and the transition to a glorified body as being raised from the dead. As the second death implies a first death, the first resurrection implies a second resurrection. While this second resurrection is not explicitly called by that name in Scripture, it is described in the following verses:

> **John 5:29** – Do not marvel at this, for an hour is coming when all who are in the tombs will hear his voice and come out, those who have done good to the resurrection of life, and those who have done evil to the resurrection of judgment.

> **Daniel 12:1-2** – At that time shall arise Michael, the great prince who has charge of your people. And there shall be a time of trouble, such as never has been since there was a nation till that time. But at that time your people shall be delivered, everyone whose name shall be found written in the book. And many of those who sleep in the dust of the earth shall awake, some to everlasting life, and some to shame and everlasting contempt.

The "resurrection of life" in John 5:29 is the "first resurrection" in Revelation 20:5-6 and the "resurrection of damnation" in John 5:29 is the second resurrection implied by Revelation 20:11-15. The verses in John and Daniel don't address the timing of each resurrection, but clearly show that there are two of them.

> cThe one who conquers will be clothed thus in white garments, and *I will never blot his name out of the book of life.* I will confess his name before my Father and before his angels. (*(emphasis mine)*

Recall that God makes clear in 1 John 5:5 that one who conquers (overcomes) is one who believes that Jesus is the Son of God. Jesus Christ is your only hope of remaining in the book of life. In fact, in the new heavens and new earth the book of life will become the "Lamb's book of life" (Rev. 21:27) because after all those who continued to refuse God's "free gift" of "eternal life through Jesus Christ" (Rom. 6:23) are blotted out it will only contain the names of those who believed in Him.

This judgment also includes "Death and Hades [16]" being cast into the lake of fire (Rev. 20:14), which corresponds precisely with the series of events laid out in 1 Corinthians 15:22-26:

> For as in Adam all die, so also in Christ shall all be made alive. But each in his own order: Christ the firstfruits, then at his coming those who belong to Christ. Then comes the end, when he delivers the kingdom to God the Father after destroying every rule and every authority and power. For he must reign until he has put all his enemies under his feet. The last enemy to be destroyed is death.

While the context here is resurrections (*i.e.* getting a perfect, immortal glorified body), the order is (1)

---

16 Hades is the holding place for the souls of unbeliever who have died; also referred to as "hell" in English.

Christ comes, (2) Christ reigns, (3) Christ delivers up the kingdom to the Father, and (4) the last enemy destroyed is death. Death will finally be destroyed when Death and Hades are cast into the lake of fire at the great white throne judgment, which follows the Millennial Kingdom and Satan's final rebellion.

New Heavens, New Earth, New Jerusalem

The canon of Scripture concludes with the final two chapters of the book of Revelation describing the new heavens, the new earth, and the new Jerusalem. The apostle Peter is given a prophecy in 2 Peter 3:10-12 that gives a little insight into the timing of this transition as well as how it will happen:

> But the day of the Lord will come like a thief, and then the heavens will pass away with a roar, and the heavenly bodies will be burned up and dissolved, and the earth and the works that are done on it will be exposed. Since all these things are thus to be dissolved, what sort of people ought you to be in lives of holiness and godliness, waiting for and hastening the coming of the day of God, because of which the heavens will be set on fire and dissolved, and the heavenly bodies will melt as they burn!

Peter refers to this dissolution of the heavens and the earth as taking place in the "day of the Lord" and the "day of God." If you recall what you read previously in this book, you will note that I said that the Day of the Lord is when Jesus will return bodily to the earth. Moreover, it makes sense to infer that the Day of the Lord will continue at least through the Millennial Kingdom. While 2 Peter 3:10-12 is not particularly specific about the chronology of the new heavens and new earth, the flow of topics in Revelation 20 through 22 indicates that this transition will take place after the great white throne judgment.

Revelation 21 and 22 provide the details of the new heavens and new earth and I encourage you to read them regularly. It is a blessing to know what good things are in store for those who are saved through faith in Christ. Here is a summary of just some of those blessings:

- the holy city, new Jerusalem, will come down from heaven (Rev. 21:2, 10-27)
- God will dwell with mankind, they will be His people, He will be their God (Rev. 21:3)
- no more death, sorrow, crying, or pain (Rev. 21:4)
- no more sinners (Rev. 21:27)
- no more curse (Rev. 22:3)
- no more sea (Rev. 21:1)
- no night, no need of a candle or the sun or moon because the glory of God, the Lamb, will be the light (Rev. 21:23, Rev. 22:5)
- the pure river of water of life and the tree of life will be there (Rev. 22:1:2)
- no temple: "its temple is the Lord God the Almighty and the Lamb" (Rev. 21:22)
- the throne of God and the Lamb will be there (Rev. 22:3)

The new heavens, new earth, and new Jerusalem will be an eternal glorious future with God for all those who are in Christ.

In Isaiah 65, verses 20-25 describe the characteristics of the Millennial Kingdom. However, just prior to this, in verses 17-19, it states that God will create new heavens and a new earth. Placing these two descriptions together in this order is God telling us *who* He is; that He is the one who will someday *create* a new heaven and a new earth, so therefore, it is no problem for Him to make some drastic changes to the current earth in the meantime.

This is not the only place in the Bible where the author states something more difficult to accomplish than the thing being promised in order to validate that that promise will be accomplished as well. The best example of this is probably Jeremiah 32:17-44, where it begins with "Ah, Lord GOD! It is you who have made the heavens and the earth by your great power and by your outstretched arm! Nothing is too hard for you," and proceeds then to explains the things He will do for Israel, also claiming "Behold, I am the LORD, the God of all flesh. Is anything too hard for me?" Zechariah 12 is another example of this. It begins by stating that the Lord "stretched out the heavens and founded the earth and formed the spirit of man within him," and then says how He will "make Jerusalem a cup of staggering to all the surrounding peoples" and other things He will bring to pass in the Tribulation. The creation of the heavens and the earth did not take place when the things prophesied in these passages from Jeremiah and Zechariah came to pass. They are statements of

138

God's power indicating that He has the power to bring about the things He is prophesying as evidenced by what He has already done.

It would be contradictory to conflate the Millennial Kingdom with the new heavens and new earth because of what we know about each of these in other passages of Scripture. For example, since there will be people with natural physical bodies that have not been glorified with the immortal and incorruptible qualities outlined in 1 Corinthians 15:50-54, they will still be given in marriage and be capable of having children (Deut. 30:5, Isa. 65:23, Jer. 30:19, Ez. 37:25, Ez. 47:22). However, everyone inhabiting the new heavens and new earth will have a glorified body and will be like the angels, who don't marry or have offspring (Lk. 20:34-35, 1 Cor. 15:50). People with unglorified bodies will still sin during the Millennial Kingdom (Isa. 2:4, Isa. 65:20, Zech. 14:18-19, Rev. 20:7-9), but there will be no sin in the new heavens and new earth (Lk. 20:36, 1 Cor. 15:52-56). Finally, even though they can live very long lives like pre-flood people, in the Millennial Kingdom, people with unglorified bodies can still die (Isa. 65:20), but there will be no death in the new heavens and new earth (Lk. 20:36, 1 Cor. 15:52-56, Rev. 21:3-4). Therefore, the Millennial Kingdom and the new heavens and new earth are different time periods.

Table 2 is designed to show the connections between the themes found in Bible prophecies of a glorious future and the eschatological events of the gathering of Israel, the Millennial Kingdom, the Day of the Lord, and Jubilee. A final column is included in the table to indicate where the prophetic theme is referenced in the New Testament. One of the things that makes the

study of End Times more difficult is that the details
are spread throughout the Scriptures. Hopefully,
this table will help with the understanding of how
these ideas fit together. Take the time to look up each
Scripture reference, considering the context and the
intent of God's purpose in what He has revealed to us.
This table illustrates how central the passages about
Israel being gathered are to Bible prophecy.

Table 2. *Prophetic Themes by Event*

Prophetic Theme	Gathered from Nations	Millennial Kingdom	Day of the Lord	Jubilee	NT Reference
You shall be my people, and I will be your God	Jer.30:22, 31:33, 32:38; Ez. 11:20, 34:30-31, 36:28, 37:23, 27; Zech. 8:8	Hos. 2:23			Heb. 8:20, (Rev. 21:3 NH/NE)
Israel will dwell safely	Jer. 23:6, 32:37; Ez. 28:26, 34:25, 27-28, 39:26	Hos. 2:18, Zech. 14:11	Zech. 14:11	Lev. 25:18-19	
In "the land" or "own land" – each tribe of Israel in their own lot	Deut. 30:;, Jer. 3:16, 18, 23:3,8, 30:3, 32:41, 33:7, 11; Ez. 11:17, 20:42, 28:25, 34:13, 36:24, 28, 37:21, 25; Amos 9:15	Ez. 45:1, 8, 47:21, 48:1-7, 22-29		Lev. 25:10	
Israel will keep God statutes	Deut. 30:8; Jer. 3:17; Ez. 11:20, 36:27, 37:23-24; Zeph. 3:13	Ez. 43:11		Lev. 25:18	

Table 2. *Prophetic Themes by Event (Continued)*

Prophetic Theme	Gathered from Nations	Millennial Kingdom	Day of the Lord	Jubilee	NT Reference
Plentiful food, land and animals fruitful	Deut. 30:9; Jer. 31:12; Ez. 34:27, 29, 36:29-30; Amos 9:14; Zech. 8:12	Isa. 27:6; Joel 2:24-26		Lev. 25:19-22	
Israel will fear no more	Jer. 23:4, 30:10; Ez. 34:28; Mic. 4:4; Zeph. 3:13				
Israel won't be ashamed	Ez. 34:29; Zeph. 3:11	Joel 2:26-27; Zeph. 3:11			
Israel will multiply	Deut. 30:5; Jer. 3:16, 23:3, 30:19; Ez. 36:37, 37:26	Zech. 10:8			
Physical healing	Jer. 30:17; Ez. 34:16	Isa. 35:5-6	Isa. 30:26		

Table 2. *Prophetic Themes by Event (Continued)*

Prophetic Theme	Gathered from Nations	Millennial Kingdom	Day of the Lord	Jubilee	NT Reference
Israel a priase & blessing on the earth, no longer a curse or byword among nations, sanctified before nations	Jer. 33:9; Ez. 20:41, 28:25, 34:28, 37:28, 39:27; Zeph. 3:19-20; Zech. 8:13	Isa. 61:9, 62:7; Joel 2:19; Zeph. 3:20			
God will circumcise heart, give new heart, write law on heart, give one heart	Deut. 30:6; Jer. 31:33, 32:39-40; Ez. 11:19, 36:26				Heb. 8:10
New covenant/ everlasting covenant	Jer. 31:31, 32:40; Ez. 20:37, 34:25, 37:26	Hos. 2:18			Rom. 11:25-27; Heb. 8:10-13, 10:16
The Lord will cleanse Israel from all iniquity and pardon them	Jer. 33:8				Rom. 11:26-27; Heb. 8:12, 10:17

Table 2. *Prophetic Themes by Event (Continued)*

Prophetic Theme	Gathered from Nations	Millennial Kingdom	Day of the Lord	Jubilee	NT Reference
Loathe yourself for evils committed, mourn for sin	Ez. 20:43, 36:31		Zech. 12:10-14 with Zech. 14:1-2	Lev. 23:27, 29, 32 with Lev. 25:9	Mt. 24:30; Rev. 1:7
The Lord will rejoice over Israel	Deut. 30:9; Jer. 32:41; Zeph. 3:17				
The Lord will turn away Israel's captivity; liberty to the captives	Deut. 30:3; Jer. 29:14; Zeph. 3:20			Lev. 25:10	
The Lord will give Israel pastors/ shepherds and feed them with knowledge and understanding	Jer. 3:15, 23:4, 31:10; Ez. 34:13-15, 23-24, 37:24; Zeph. 3:13				

Table 2. *Prophetic Themes by Event (Continued)*

Prophetic Theme	Gathered from Nations	Millennial Kingdom	Day of the Lord	Jubilee	NT Reference
The Lord will be in Jerusalem reigning as King over Israel and all the earth; throne of His glory; David's throne	Jer. 3:17, 23:5; Ez. 37:22; Zeph. 3:15; Zech. 8:3, 21-23	Isa. 2:3-4, 12:6; Ez. 43:7, 9, 48:35; Joel 3:17; Mic. 4:2-3, 7, 5:15	Joel 3:14-16; Zech. 14:3-4, 9		Mt. 19;28, 25:31; Lk. 1:32; Acts 2:30; Rev. 20:4, 6
The Lord will curse/punish/purge out Israel's enemies, punish the wicked with fury and fierce anger; destroy sinners out of the land; day of vengeance; cruel wrath; destruction	Deut. 30:7; Jer. 30:16, 20, 23; Ez. 20:33-34, 38, 28:26, 34:16-17; Zeph. 3:11	Isa. 11:4, 34:2-3, 8, 35:4; Joel 3:17	Isa. 13:5-6, 9, 11, 13, 30:26-28; Jer. 46:10; Joel 1:15; 3:14-16; Zeph. 1:2-18; Zech. 14:12		Mt. 13:41; Lk. 21:22; 2 Thes. 1:8-9; Rev. 6:17, 11:18, 16:19, 19:15, 21

Table 2. *Prophetic Themes by Event (Continued)*

Prophetic Theme	Gathered from Nations	Millennial Kingdom	Day of the Lord	Jubilee	NT Reference
Idols cut off out of the land	Ez. 36:25, 37:23		Isa. 2:18, 20; Zech. 13:2; Mic. 5:13		
Clouds, thick darkness, gloominess	Ez. 34:12		Ez. 30:3; Joel 2:1-2; Amos 5:18, 20		
Sun, moon, and stars darkened			Isa. 13:10; Joel 2:10, 31, 3:15		Mt. 24:29-31; Mk. 13:24-26; Lk. 21:25-27
Hearts will melt with fear			Isa. 13:7-8		Lk. 21:26

Several passages of Scripture are written using a chiastic structure. [17] This is speculation, but consider the idea that God may have arranged world history in a chiastic pattern as follows:

A – Eternity Past (triune God only, perfection)

B – The Garden of Eden, before the fall of man, but potential for childbearing, sin, and death

C – From the Fall until the Flood (the Days of Noah, wickedness in all the earth)

D – From the Flood to the giving of the Law on Mt. Sinai (not under The Law)

X – The Nation of Israel (From the giving of the Law to the giving of the Spirit at Pentecost; under The Law, when Jesus Christ came to redeem fallen mankind – *the highlight of history*! In chiastic poetry the main point is in the middle section)

D' – From the giving of the Spirit at Pentecost until the Tribulation (not under The Law; under grace)

C' – The Tribulation (70th Week of Daniel's prophecy, like the days of Noah, wickedness in all the earth)

B' – The Millennial Kingdom (restoration/regeneration, but still childbearing, sin, and death)

A' – New Heavens & New Earth (eternity future, the triune God and all His saints and holy angels, no more sin, no more curse)

---

17 *https://en.wikipedia.org/wiki/Chiastic_structure*

The Rapture

Now that we have worked our way through the End Time events chronologically, let's turn our attention to one more important piece of the prophetic puzzle: the Rapture.

What is the Rapture?

The Rapture is most clearly defined in 1 Thessalonians 4:15-17:

> For this we declare to you by a word from the Lord, that we who are alive, who are left until the coming of the Lord, will not precede those who have fallen asleep. For the Lord himself will descend from heaven with a cry of command, with the voice of an archangel, and with the sound of the trumpet of God. And the dead in Christ will rise first. Then we who are alive, who are left, will be caught up together with them in the clouds to meet the Lord in the air, and so we will always be with the Lord.

In the New Testament, the state of believers who have died is described as being asleep since their spirit is still alive and well (Acts 7:60, Acts 13:36, 1 Cor. 15:6, 18-20, 51). Another passage that describes the Rapture is 1 Cor. 15:51-55:

> Behold! I tell you a mystery. We shall not all sleep, but we shall all be changed, in a moment, in the twinkling of an eye, at the last trumpet. For the trumpet will sound, and the dead will be raised

imperishable, and we shall be changed. For this perishable body must put on the imperishable, and this mortal body must put on immortality. When the perishable puts on the imperishable, and the mortal puts on immortality, then shall come to pass the saying that is written: "Death is swallowed up in victory. O death, where is your victory? O death, where is your sting?"

Table 3 shows this passage harmonized with 1 Thessalonians 14:13-18 to highlight the parallels.

Table 3. *Parallels of the Key Points of the Rapture from 1 Thessalonians 4:15-18 and 1 Corinthians 15:51-55.*

1 Thes. 14:15-18	1 Cor. 15:51-55
we who are alive, who are left until the coming of the Lord	we shall not all sleep (*die*)
with the sound of the trumpet of God	at the last trumpet: for the trumpet will sound
the dead in Christ will rise first	the dead will be raised imperishable
then we who are alive, who are left, will be caught up together with them in the clouds to meet the Lord in the air	and we shall be changed
we do not want you to be uninformed, brothers, about those who are asleep (*dead*), that you may not grieve as others do who have no hope	death is swallowed up in victory
encourage one another with these words	O death, where is your sting? O grave, where is your victory?

John 14:1-3 also contains characteristics of the Rapture:

Let not your hearts be troubled. Believe in God; believe also in me. In my Father's house are many

150

rooms. If it were not so, would I have told you that I go to prepare a place for you? And if I go and prepare a place for you, *I will come again and will take you to myself, that where I am you may be also. (emphasis mine)*

While the disciples Jesus was speaking to would not have known the sudden and supernatural nature of the rapture as it is described in 1 Thessalonians 4:17, they were given a comforting promise that Jesus would come back for them and receive them to Himself so that they would always be with Him after that. They were not told the mechanism of the Rapture at that time, but they got the point that Jesus would come back for them. They will be in the group that Paul calls the "dead in Christ" who will rise first (1 Thes. 4:16).

At the moment of the Rapture God will provide all believers who have previously died and all believers who are alive with a glorified body that is incorruptible and immortal like the one that He took on at His resurrection (1 Cor. 15:51-57, Phil. 3:21, 1 Jn. 3:2). This will take place in the "twinkling of an eye" – an *atomos* [18] of time – in an instant. This body will be like the body that Jesus obtained at His resurrection, which is why He is called the "firstfruits of those who have fallen asleep" in 1 Corinthians 15:20. Once in this glorified body, we will no longer be in the flesh, which is contrary to the Spirit (Gal. 5:18) and where sin dwells (Rom. 7:18), and so we will no longer sin ever again nor be capable of dying!

---

18 *Atomos* is the transliteration of the Greek for "moment" in 1 Corinthians 15:52.

The Greek word translated as "caught up" in 1 Thessalonians 4:17 is *harpazo*. The word we use, Rapture, is derived from the Latin word *rapiemur*. This is the word used in place of *harpazo*, for example in the *Latin Vulgate* translated by Jerome. To get a sense of the meaning of a word and gain insight as to how the Holy Spirit uses a given word, it is useful to see where else it is used in the Bible. *Harpazo* is used in 11 different forms in 13 verses in the New Testament. In three of those uses it refers to something or someone being taken by force, such as in the following verses:

> **Matthew 11:12** – From the days of John the Baptist until now the kingdom of heaven has suffered violence, and the violent *take it by force. (emphasis mine)*

> **John 6:15** – Perceiving then that they were about to come and *take him by force* to make him king, Jesus withdrew again to the mountain by himself. *(emphasis mine)*

> **Acts 23:10** – And when the dissension became violent, the tribune, afraid that Paul would be torn to pieces by them, commanded the soldiers to go down and *take him away from among them by force* and bring him into the barracks. *(emphasis mine)*

In the explanation of the parable of the sower in Matthew 13:19, Jesus tells His disciples the following:

> When anyone hears the word of the kingdom and does not understand it, the evil one comes and *snatches away* what has been sown in his

152

heart. This is what was sown along the path. *(emphasis mine)*

The word *harpazo* describes how Satan snatches God's Word from the hearts of those who heard it. In John 10:28-29, Jesus describes how believers are secure in Himself and in the Father:

> I give them eternal life, and they will never perish, and no one will *snatch* them out of my hand. My Father, who has given them to me, is greater than all, and no one is able to *snatch* them out of the Father's hand. *(emphasis mine)*

Harpazo is translated as plucking us out of God's hand. This implies a quick motion to grab something. This is seen in its usage in Jude 1:22-23 as well.

> **Jude 1:22-23** – And have mercy on those who doubt; save others by *snatching* them out of the fire; to others show mercy with fear, hating even the garment stained by the flesh. *(emphasis mine)*

Notice in many of these uses that the quickness of the motion is due to the urgency to rescue someone from danger. Uses of *harpazo* that are more similar to its use in 1 Thessalonians 4:17, which defines the Rapture, are in the following verses.

> **Acts 8:39** – And when they came up out of the water, the Spirit of the Lord *carried* Philip *away*, and the eunuch saw him no more, and went on his way rejoicing. *(emphasis mine)*

> **2 Corinthians 12:2** – I know a man in Christ who fourteen years ago was *caught up* to the third heaven — whether in the body or out of the body I do not know, God knows. *(emphasis mine)*

> **Revelation 12:5** – She gave birth to a male child, one who is to rule all the nations with a rod of iron, but her child was *caught up* to God and to his throne. *(emphasis mine)*

In each of the three previous examples a person is supernaturally translated from one location to another.

With the idea of the Rapture revealed in the New Testament, there are some Old Testament verses that lend support to it. Consider the following.

> **Genesis 5:24** – Enoch walked with God: and he was not; for God took him.

> **2 Kings 2:11** – And as they still went on and talked, behold, chariots of fire and horses of fire separated the two of them. And Elijah went up by a whirlwind into heaven.

Aside from Enoch, everyone else listed in the generations of Adam in Genesis 5 are specifically said to have *died*. In contrast, the Bible says that God *took* Enoch. Genesis 5:24 and 2 Kings 2:11 are two cases of a person being supernaturally translated from the earth to heaven. The following verses speak of God's people being hidden from something.

> **Isaiah 26:20-21** – Come, my people, enter your chambers, and shut your doors behind you; hide yourselves for a little while until the fury has passed by. For behold, the LORD is coming out from his place to punish the inhabitants of the earth for their iniquity, and the earth will

154

disclose the blood shed on it, and will no more cover its slain. [19]

The "fury" referred to in Isaiah 26:20 is a phrase that in some passages of Scripture refers to the Tribulation and the return of the Lord and is also translated as the indignation (Isa. 34:2, Dan. 8:19, Dan. 11:36). Notice here, too, that the LORD will come to punish the earth *after* this fury/indignation. This corresponds to the Second Coming of Jesus that is described in Revelation 19:11-21, which occurs immediately after the seven-year Tribulation. Before Jesus returns to punish the earth, God calls his people to hide in their chambers. Could these chambers be what Jesus has gone to prepare for us (Jn. 14:2-3)?

Isaiah 57:1 – The righteous man perishes, and no one lays it to heart; devout men are taken away, while no one understands. *For the righteous man is taken away from calamity. (emphasis mine)*

Is the "calamity" a reference to the Tribulation?

Joel 2:15-16 – Blow the trumpet in Zion; consecrate a fast; call a solemn assembly; gather the people. Consecrate the congregation; assemble the elders; gather the children, even nursing infants. *Let the bridegroom leave his room, and the bride her chamber. (emphasis mine)*

Taking Joel 2:16 together with Isaiah 26:20 stated above, God's people, the bride, will be released from her

---

19 Isaiah 26:19 can be seen as a veiled reference to the resurrection (compare with Mt. 27:52-53 and Rom 6:4-5), so in three consecutive verses you have the resurrection or Christ, the Rapture, and the Second Coming.

chamber to return with Jesus at His Second Coming. Revelation 19:7-9 describes this exact situation, with the wife of the Lamb being arrayed in fine linen, which is called "the righteous deeds of the saints." Moreover, Jesus told His disciplesin John 14:3 that He was going to His Father's house in heaven to "prepare a place" for them. Could that refer to the chamber where the bride will stay during the Tribulation?

> **Zeph. 2:3** – Seek the LORD, all you humble of the land, who do his just commands; seek righteousness; seek humility; perhaps you may be hidden on the day of the anger of the LORD.

Much like Isaiah 26:20-21 stated above, the reference in Zephaniah 2:3 to the "day of the anger of the LORD" can refer to the day that Jesus returns in person to judge the earth – the Day of the Lord (Isa: 13:9). There is a thread running through these verses of God's people being protected by being removed before a severe judgment comes on the earth. We are told in 1 Thessalonians 5:9 that "For God has not destined us for wrath, but to obtain salvation through our Lord Jesus Christ."

When is the Rapture?

While the Rapture itself will be an instantaneous event, the timing of when this will take place in relation to the other eschatological events is difficult to discern. However, the Bible gives some compelling reasons to conclude that the Rapture will occur prior to the seven-year Tribulation (70th week of the prophecy given in Daniel 9:24-27). Let's consider a few passages of Scripture to see why this might be so.

156

The context in the verses that most clearly define the Rapture, 1 Thessalonians 4:13-18, is that God will "bring with" Jesus the "dead in Christ" and believers who are "alive, who are left" will be caught up together with them in the clouds to meet the Lord in the air" and be with Him forever. In order to bring the ones who are caught up with Him when He comes, what order must these two events happen in? Logically, it means that they must be caught up in the air before Jesus returns to the earth.

In 1 Thessalonians 5:1-11, which of course follows chapter 4, Paul is explaining to the Thessalonian church that the Day of the Lord will come with sudden destruction as a thief in the night on unbelievers but *not* on those who believe in Christ. It is in this passage that God says believers are "not destined for wrath" (v. 9). Would these words be very comforting (v. 11) if the Thessalonian readers at the time understood that God's wrath and judgment on the world would be suddenly poured out on the earth while they were on it, and only afterward would He catch them up to Himself? It is only if you are not watchful and don't repent that the Day of the Lord will come on you as a thief (Rev. 3:3, Rev. 16:15). While it is true that Christians will suffer persecution in this life (2 Tim. 3:12, Jn. 15:18-20, Jn. 6:33), we are not destined for God's wrath.

Moving to 2 Thessalonians, before the man of sin (the Antichrist) is revealed there must first be a "rebellion" (2 Thes. 2:3). The word "rebellion" is an English rendering of the Greek noun *apostasia*, which can be understood as either a spiritual departure or a physical departure, depending on the context. Most of the common modern English versions translate *apostasia* in this verse as falling away, apostasy, or rebellion. However, the Wycliffe (1384), Tyndale (1526), Coverdale (1535), Cranmer, Breeches (1576), Beza (1583), and the Geneva (1608) Bible translate it as a physical departure. The motivation for the change to doctrinal departure came when the Catholic Rheims Bible (1576) used "Protestant Revolt" and the King James Bible (1611) used "falling away." [20] While this is a minority view in the Bible translations of today, the 2018 booklet by Dr. Andy Woods titled The Falling Away: Spiritual Departure or Physical Rapture? A second Look at Thessalonians 2:3 provides other engaging arguments for this being a physical departure. Second Thessalonians 2:1 sets the context for a physical departure in that he is clarifying things about "the coming of our Lord Jesus Christ, and our being gathered together to him," which involves a physical movement from one place to another, not a doctrinal departure. If this is the correct interpretation of this verse, then the Rapture must occur before the Tribulation.

If 1 Thessalonians 4:13-18 and 2 Thessalonians 2:1-13 are covering the same material and, as 2 Thessalonians 2:5 claims, that Paul taught the newly planted church in Thessalonica about the Rapture and the coming of the Lord when he was with them in person and then was writing again to remind the of these things, then you can see that the combined

---

20 Woods, *The Falling Away: Spiritual Departure or Physical Rapture? A second Look at Thessalonians 2:3*, pp. 38-39.

message in both passages is that believers will be caught up (raptured) before the coming of the Lord because they will be returning with Him when He comes and that this departure (rapture) will occur before the Antichrist is revealed to the world.

Continuing to verses 6 through 8 in 2 Thessalonians 2, a restrainer will be removed before the wicked one (Antichrist) is revealed to the world. Who or what is this restrainer? One very reasonable view is that the one restraining the Antichrist is the Holy Spirit working through the church. This occurs through true Christians in positions of power and authority who work to stop wicked laws, rules, and policies and govern in a godly manner. It also happens when people around you will behave better and refrain from using foul language just because you are there (if you are a Christian and those around you know it), even if you don't say anything about it. If 2 Thessalonians 2:3 is saying the church will depart in the Rapture before the Antichrist is revealed, then 2 Thessalonians 2:6-8 is consistent with this in saying that the Holy Spirit will no longer be restraining the Antichrist through the church when the time comes for him to be revealed.

Chapters 2 and 3 of Revelation contain letters to seven churches with promises to those who overcome and each letter saying. "He that hath an ear, let him hear what the Spirit saith unto the churches" (Rev. 2:7, 11, 17, 29, Rev. 3:6, 13, 22). The Bible defines overcoming as believing that Jesus is the Son of God (1 Jn. 5:5). A promise in the letter to the church in Philadelphia is given in Revelation 3:10 as:

> Because you have kept my word about patient
> endurance, I will keep you from the hour of trial
> that is coming on the whole world, to try those
> who dwell on the earth.

This hour of trial is a time of a worldwide testing. Luke
21:34-36 says it this way:

> But watch yourselves lest your hearts be
> weighed down with dissipation and drunkenness
> and cares of this life, and that day come upon
> you suddenly like a trap. For it will come upon
> all who dwell on the face of the whole earth. But
> stay awake at all times, praying that you may have
> strength to escape all these things that are going
> to take place, and to stand before the Son of Man.

In some ancient manuscripts (such as the ones the
King James Bible is based on), the phrase "you may
have strength to escape" instead reads as "accounted
worthy to escape." As I understand the issue, this is a
better fit. If you are wondering who is worthy to escape
and who are the righteous who will be taken away
from the evil to come, then you are asking a very good
question. No one is worthy in and of themselves. As
Christians, our worthiness and righteousness come
only from our Savior Jesus Christ (Phil. 3:9). On the
other hand, if it should really be about our strength
to escape, as Christians our strength comes from the
Lord (1 Tim. 1:12).

If you are wondering who it is that has kept the
Lord's word about "patient endurance" in Revelation
3:10, consider that as Jesus prayed to the Father for
His disciples the night before His crucifixion, He said

160

that they had kept the Father's word. While keeping God's word through our obedience should be our aim, we fall short in our fleshly state. But God accounts us as keeping His word because we are in Christ by faith. Therefore, we will be kept out of this trial that will one day come upon the whole world.

The Olivet Discourse concludes with the Lord separating sheep and goats after He returns to the earth (Mt. 25:31:46). If the Rapture were to coincide with the coming of Christ to earth at the beginning of the Day of the Lord, why would such a separation of sheep and goats be necessary? Isn't the Rapture itself a separation of believers and unbelievers? The Rapture occurs in the twinkling of an eye (1 Cor. 15:52), whereas the separation of sheep and goats contains conversations between the Lord Jesus and the people and so must require some time to play out.

In Matthew 24:37-39 and Luke 17:26-27, Jesus says that the coming of the Son of man will be like the days of Noah. He specifically points out that people in Noah's day were "eating and drinking, marrying and giving in marriage until the day when Noah entered the ark," and the flood came and destroyed them all. Noah and his family entered the ark, and it was seven days before the fountains of the deep broke open and the flood came (Gen. 7:10). Could these seven days preceding the flood possibly be a foreshadowing that correspond to the seven years of Tribulation that will precede Jesus' return to judge the earth?

Following this, in Matthew 24:40-41 Jesus says that when the Son of man comes:

> Then two men will be in the field; one will be taken and one left. Two women will be grinding at the mill; one will be taken and one left.

These verses have sometimes been interpreted as describing the Rapture because when the Rapture occurs there will certainly be some taken and some left, but when the flood of Noah's day occurred it was the unbelievers who were taken away and the believers (Noah and his family) who remained because they were safe in the ark. Note also that Jesus is likening the flood to His return, not the Rapture. When He returns, He will remove all of those who do not trust in Him and leave on earth the people who do (Mt. 13:41, Mt. 25:31-46, Mt. 24:22).

Luke 17:28-30 records Jesus comparing the coming of the Son of man to the days of Lot:

> Likewise, just as it was in the days of Lot — they were eating and drinking, buying and selling, planting and building, but on the day when Lot went out from Sodom, fire and sulfur rained from heaven and destroyed them all — so will it be on the day when the Son of Man is revealed.

The Bible says that one of the two angels who came to bring judgment on the cities of Sodom and Gomorrah told Lot that they could not do anything to destroy the cities until Lot had come out of them (Gen. 19:22). Doesn't this imply that the Rapture must occur sometime *before* the Lord returns to judge the earth?

What people group is the 70 weeks prophecy for? Why is the Tribulation called a "time of distress for Jacob" in Jeremiah ? What will happen after the

162

"fullness of the Gentiles" of Romans 11:25 has come in? According to Daniel 9:24, the angel Gabriel told Daniel that seventy weeks were decreed upon his people. Who are Daniel's people? Jews. The children of Israel. So, just as the first 69 weeks of seven years each specifically pertained to the Jewish people, the 70th week, which is the Tribulation period, must also be specifically for Israel and not Gentiles. A distinction between Israel and Gentiles is made in Romans 11 regarding a future time period when God's focus shifts from initially being on Israel, then to Gentiles, and then back to Israel. In the imagery of an olive tree Israel is the initial tree but then branches are broken off due to unbelief and Gentile branches are grafted in. Eventually, however, when the "fullness of the Gentiles" comes in, Israel will be grafted back into that tree so that their "fullness" can be realized (Rom. 11:12, 23-25). These three seemingly distinct passages tell the same story, that there will come a time when God will bring His attention back to Israel as a people and that this will occur in the seven-year Tribulation. The removal of the church, which currently consists of some Jews but mostly Gentiles, may be God's way of making that transition.

As mentioned previously, people can still have children (Deut. 30:5, Isa. 65:23, Jer. 30:19, Ez. 37:25, Ez. 47:22), can still sin (Deut. 30:7, Isa. 2:4, Isa. 65:20, Rev. 20:7-9), and still die during the Millennial Kingdom (Isa. 65:20). It is also true that at the moment of the Rapture the bodies of believers are immediately changed to glorified bodies that do not reproduce (Lk. 20:35), cannot sin (1 Cor. 15:52-56), and cannot die

(Lk. 20:36, 1 Cor. 15:52-56). If the Rapture coincides with the return of Jesus at the end of the Tribulation, then all believers would be given glorified bodies and there would be no people left with natural bodies that can have children, sin, and die during the Millennial Kingdom. On the other hand, if all believers on earth are caught up before the Tribulation so that it begins with only unbelievers in natural, unglorified bodies, people that come to faith in Christ and live through the Tribulation to enter into the Millennial Kingdom will have natural bodies and therefore will still have the capacity for childbirth, sin, and death during the kingdom age.

The word choices and order of events in the book of Revelation also lend support to the idea of a pre-tribulation Rapture. In chapters 1-3, the words church or churches are used to describe believers in Christ a total of 18 times (in the English Standard Version) and there are no occurrences of the words saint or saints. Revelation 4:1 says this:

> After this I looked, and behold, a door standing open in heaven! And the first voice, which I had heard speaking to me *like a trumpet*, said, *"Come up here,* and I will show you what must take place after this." *(emphasis mine)*

The rest of chapter 4 and all of chapter 5 describe the incredible majesty and glory of what John sees in heaven and sets the context for the unsealing of the seven-sealed scroll that describes what will take place during the seven-year Tribulation, which is detailed in Revelation chapters 6 through 18. The word church

164

or churches is never used in these chapters. Instead, believers in Christ are called the saints, which is frequently used in the Scriptures to refer to those who are saved. At the very least, a distinction is made in Revelation in the word used to describe believers during that time period. The New Testament refers to believers using both church and saints, while the Old Testament refers to believers as saints many times but never as the church. Jesus instituted the use of the word church to refer to believers in Matthew 16:18. In each of the letters to the seven churches found in Revelation 2 and 3, you can find the sentence, "He who has an ear, let him hear what the Spirit says to the churches" (Rev. 2:7, 11, 17, 29, Rev. 3:6, 13, 22). However, a similar statement in Revelation 13:9 says only, "If anyone has an ear, let him hear." There is no mention of the churches. Is this a literary way to indicate that the church will not be present on earth during this time?

Some verses say that no one but God the Father knows the Day of the Lord's return — at least at the time that these verses were written (*e.g.* Mt. 24:36, Acts 1:7), but other verses imply that the day will be able to be determined from chronological information in the Bible once certain events take place. For example, Jesus should return seven years after the Antichrist confirms a seven-year covenant with Israel and 1260 days from when the Antichrist causes the daily sacrifice to cease and sets up the abomination of desolation in the holy place (Dan. 9:27 with Mt. 24:15, Dan. 7:25, Dan. 12:7, Rev. 13:5). A pre-tribulation Rapture resolves the tension between people knowing and not knowing the day of the Second Coming. In the Olivet Discourse, Jesus told His disciples, And "what I say to you I say to all: Stay awake" (Mk. 13:37) and commanded them to watch (Mt. 25:13). The Scriptures were written for all of mankind, which necessarily includes:

1. saints who will be raptured or die before the Day of the Lord takes place so they can't know the day,

2. people who come to faith during the seven years of Tribulation and so they can determine the day by studying the Bible, and

3. all of those who never believe, who can't know the day if they die prior to the Tribulation and won't know the day if they are in the Tribulation because they are in darkness.

Also consider that if you "watch yourselves" the day won't come upon you unawares (Lk. 21:34) and you *won't* be found sleeping (Mk. 13:32-37). It is only if you are not watchful and don't repent that the Day of the Lord will come on you as a thief (Rev. 3:3, Rev. 16:15). Servants found watching when the master returns will be blessed while those not watching will be cut in pieces and placed with the unfaithful (Lk. 12:35-48). These exhortations are given in the passages of Scripture that speak about the Tribulation period. The Day of the Lord will come as sudden destruction and as a thief in the night on the unbelievers in the Tribulation because they have no spiritual discernment and are described as being in darkness, asleep, and of the night (1 Thes. 5:1-7).

The New Testament encourages Christians to look for Jesus while we await His return. Here are three verses to illustrate this:

Philippians 3:20 – But our citizenship is in heaven, and from it we await a Savior, the Lord Jesus Christ.

1 Thessalonians 1:10 – And to wait for his Son from heaven, whom he raised from the dead, Jesus who delivers us from the wrath to come.

Titus 2:13 – Waiting for our blessed hope, the appearing of the glory of our great God and Savior Jesus Christ.

The New Testament does not exhort Christians to look for the antichrist to confirm a seven-year covenant with Israel or for two witnesses in Jerusalem. We are given hope and comfort and inspired to live godly lives as we look for Jesus to come for us. The point here is that the Rapture is imminent. It could occur at any moment. There are no prophecies that need to be fulfilled in order for the Rapture to occur.

It may be tempting to think that the Rapture and the Day of the Lord will take place simultaneously because there are a few similarities. For example, Jesus is the central figure, there is a trumpet, there are clouds, and believers are gathered. However, there are some very stark differences as well. The Day of the Lord is a day of judgment and vengeance (Isa, 13:9-11, Jer. 46:10, Rev. 19:11) whereas the Rapture is a day that brings comfort with resurrection as a theme (1 Thes. 4:16-18, 1 Cor. 15:51-52). The Day of the Lord will be preceded by signs, such as the events of the seven-year Tribulation, while the Rapture is imminent.

The fact that clouds are mentioned in conjunction with the return of the Lord and with the Rapture does not make them the same event. God went with Israel in the Exodus in a "pillar of a cloud" in the day (Ex. 13:21), the Lord descended in a cloud on Mount Sinai (Ex. 34:5), the glory of the Lord appearing as a cloud has filled the tabernacle and the temple at times (Ex. 40:34, 1 Ki. 8:11), and a cloud received Jesus when He ascended to heaven (Acts 1:9). The point is, God is often accompanied by clouds when He is interacting with man. The clouds are not restricted to only the Day of the Lord and the Rapture.

Similarly, just because a trumpet is blown at both the return of the Lord and at the Rapture doesn't mean that they are the same event because there are many trumpets blown for a variety of reasons throughout the Bible. A good place to begin studying trumpets in the Bible is Numbers 10:1-10. These verses say that God commanded Moses to have two silver trumpets made and goes on to explain how they were to be used. These uses include calling the assembly and the moving of camp (same concept as the Rapture), sounding an alarm for war so that God will remember them and save them from their enemies (same concept as the Day of the Lord), as part of priestly ordinances and blown over sacrifices of burnt offerings and peace offerings in the beginnings of months as a memorial before God. They are also instructed to blow these trumpets on days of gladness and in solemn days. Beyond Numbers 10:1-10, there are many references to trumpets in the Bible, some made of silver, and some are made from the horn of an animal, such as a ram. The point here is that there are so many uses of a trumpet in Scripture that a trumpet accompanying an event, such as the Rapture or the Day of the Lord, does not by itself indicate that they are the same event.

This is a good place to address the "last trumpet" of 1 Corinthians 15:52 and the seventh trumpet in Revelation 11:15. Are these referring to the same trumpet? The passage in 1 Corinthians 15:50-58 is an account of the Rapture and coincides with 1 Thessalonians 4:13-18 as we covered previously. The description in 1 Thessalonians 4:16 calls the trumpet that accompanies the Rapture the "trumpet of God." The seven trumpets in Revelation are given to angels and the seventh trumpet is blown by an angel (Rev. 8:2, 11:15). Calling the trumpet in 1 Corinthians 15:52 the "last trumpet" may not mean that it is the last trumpet blast ever to be, but that it is the last trumpet to be blown during the church age and the trumpet that ushers in the end of the age.

Time Gap?

It is likely that there will be some time gap between the Rapture and the beginning of the Tribulation. It will not be a very long time gap because the state of the world will get really bad very rapidly without the restraining influence that Christians have on unbelievers by the power of the Holy Spirit. The Rapture is tied to the church, not Israel. The Tribulation period (70th week of Daniel's prophecy) is specifically for Israel, not the church. There is nothing specific in the Bible that says there will be any kind of time gap between the Rapture and the Tribulation, so you may wonder where this idea comes from. If the events in the seven-year Tribulation and the return of the Lord are connected to the fall feast days, then the timing of these events can be determined within a given year. Since the Rapture could occur at any moment, it must not be bound to any other events. It will be the trigger that sets the other End Times events in motion.

Historically, there was a forty-year time gap between when Pentecost (feast of weeks) was fulfilled with the pouring out of the Holy Spirit in AD 30 and when the Roman general Titus and his army destroyed the temple in Jerusalem in AD 70. The Roman army brought an end to a functioning temple and Jewish society in the land. Josephus says the inner temple was taken over on Nisan 14 exactly 40 years to the day from the crucifixion of Jesus.[21] In the first transition from Israel to the church age, there was an overlap of 40 years. A short time gap between the Rapture and the Tribulation is not an unreasonable possibility.

First Coming and Second Coming: Instantaneous Events?

The Second Coming does not need to all take place in an instant - it can be spread out over years. Consider the First Coming. When did it occur? At the immaculate conception of Jesus? Was it at His birth?

21 *Chronology of the War According to Josephus Part 6, https://josephus. org/FlJosephus2/warChronology6Factions.htm*

Was it at the temple when He was twelve? Was it His public ministry? Was it the crucifixion? Resurrection? Forty days walking the earth in a glorified body? His ascension into heaven? All of these things occurred at what we might call the First Coming or First Advent of Jesus. These events took place over the course of about 34 years. Similarly, the Second Coming can be considered to include the Rapture, which will trigger the Tribulation, and then the return of Jesus bodily to judge the earth and reign for 1000 years.

Discerning the Times

Jesus has already come to the earth in the flesh in His First Advent, and with 20/20 hindsight we can see ways in which God prepared the world for it. The Bible says that God sent His Son "when the fullness of time had come" (Gal. 4:4). Historically, the Greek Empire controlled the Near and Middle East a couple of hundred hears before Christ came, spreading Greek culture and with it a common language that enables people of different languages to communicate more effectively. Following that, the Roman Empire conquered even more of the world and made long-distance travel more efficient by building a spectacular system of roads. Common language and an extensive road system facilitated the spread of the gospel from Jerusalem to Judea and Samaria and to the ends of the earth (Acts 1:8). The Romans also employed a method of capital punishment known as crucifixion, which was accurately described and prophesied in Psalm 22:16 ("they have pierced my hands and feet") about a thousand years before it was inflicted on Jesus. In fact, Jesus would have been stoned by the Jews under the charge of blasphemy (Lev. 24:10-16) but because Jewish law had been subjugated to Roman law, they were not permitted to carry out capital punishment and were forced to take the case of Jesus to the Roman governor Pontius Pilate. Because of this change in the legal structure, Jesus was crucified rather than stoned. This law imposed by the

Romans onto the Jews was part of the stage-setting for prophecy to be fulfilled.

In the Old Testament, the men of Issachar were praised for having an "understanding of the times, to know what Israel ought to do" (1 Chron. 12:32). In the New Testament, Jesus criticized the Pharisees and Sadducees for knowing how to "interpret the appearance of the sky" but not being able to "interpret the signs of the times" (Mt. 16:1-3). When explaining the signs that indicate the end of the age recorded in Matthew 24:32-33, Jesus said this:

> From the fig tree learn its lesson: as soon as its branch becomes tender and puts out its leaves, you know that summer is near. So also, when you see all these things, you know that he is near, at the very gates.

Do you see any leaves on that fig tree? Do world events seem to be aligning with Bible prophecies of the last days? I am in no way suggesting that we read today's headlines and use them to try to interpret the Bible. What I am saying is that Christians ought to read the Bible and interpret current events through the lens of a biblical worldview.

When you are aware of the outline that the sovereign God has laid out in the Bible for the events that will take place as this age comes to an end, there are some key areas where you can see how the events of the world are falling into place. Here are several ways that God is laying the groundwork for the End Times prophecies to be carried out. Within each of these categories, do you see any leaves on that fig tree that Jesus spoke of (Mt. 24:32-35)?

174

- Israel has been an internationally recognized nation since 1948 and is located in the land God promised them

- The need for a covenant/peace treaty with Israel

- All nations aligning against Israel

- Jewish temple to be built in Jerusalem

- Deception in Christ's name, false prophets, false christs

- Wars & rumors of wars

- Famines

- Pestilence (this includes any kind of illness or disease)

- The love of many will grow cold

- Earthquakes

- Fearful sights in heavens

- Romans 1:18-32 (in society)

  ☐ People suppress the knowledge of God

  ☐ Foolish hearts are darkened

  ☐ Worship of the creature rather than the Creator

  ☐ People are given over to lust, dishonorable passions, and unnatural, affections (*i.e.* homosexuality/sexual immorality/ transgenderism)

- 1 Tim. 4:1-3, 2 Tim. 3:1-5, 2 Tim 4:3-4 (in the church)

  ☐ Ungodly behaviors, including being "lovers of

self, lovers of money, proud, arrogant, abusive, disobedient to their parents, ungrateful, unholy, heartless, unappeasable, slanderous, without self-control, brutal, not loving good, treacherous, reckless, swollen with conceit, lovers of pleasure rather than lovers of God, having the appearance of godliness, but denying its power" (2 Tim. 3:2-5).

☐ Bible preachers and teachers departing from the faith to teach doctrines of demons

● Global government

● Global economy

● Global religion

● Alliances of nations for Ezekiel 38 – Russia (Rosh), Iran (Persia), Turkey (Meshech, Tubal, Gomer, Togarmah), Libya (Put), Sudan (Ethiopia or Cush), Central Asia "-stan" countries (Magog)

● Technological advancements that facilitate the entire world's ability to see the two witnesses in Jerusalem and to equip the Antichrist with tools for global control (like no buying or selling without the mark of the beast)

This is by no means an exhaustive list. Pay attention to the world around you. Watch and pray. Study the Word and spend time in fellowship with the church (fellow believers) to cultivate a biblical worldview. Seek to understand the outline for the future that God has given us. Don't take my word for it, study it for yourself with all readiness of mind (Acts 17:11, 2 Tim. 2:15).

Knowing God's plan and seeing it unfold is faith-affirming and brings comfort, especially in times when world events look scary. Let's study what God has revealed to us in the Bible, not so much for the sake of knowing the details, but so that we can know the Lord our God and have deeper fellowship with Him.

How Should We Live Knowing He is Coming?

As we eagerly await His coming, we who follow Jesus should love one another as He loves us, preach the gospel, make disciples, fight the good fight, and walk in a manner worthy to be called by His name. In doing so, we will also be a tool in the hands of the Holy Spirit in His function as the restrainer of 2 Thessalonians 2:6-7. We should serve the Lord with joy in our hearts, not being fearful but knowing that God will ultimately judge the wicked and provide a glorious future for those that love Him. The following verses say it well.

1 John 2:28 – And now, little children, abide in him, so that when he appears we may have confidence and not shrink from him in shame at his coming.

1 John 3:2-3 – Beloved, we are God's children now, and what we will be has not yet appeared; but we know that when he appears we shall be like him, because we shall see him as he is. And everyone who thus hopes in him purifies himself as he is pure.

In Luke 19:12-13, the Lord Jesus tells a parable of a nobleman who travelled to a far country to receive a kingdom and then return, whose instructions to his servants were to "Engage in business until I come". Let's take these words to heart and be active in serving the Lord until He comes!

DAVE REINEKE **179**

How Close Are We?

We've never been closer than we are today! The stage is being set for the global government, economy, and religion of the 70th week of Daniel's prophecy.

Whether it be the Rapture or that your life comes to a sudden, unexpected end you need to be ready. You need to have hope! You don't know what a day may bring (Prov. 27:1). If you have not yet done so, repent and believe the Good News! Place your faith in Jesus Christ as your Savior and be reconciled to your Creator, forgiven of all your sins, and redeemed!

Some of My Favorite Resources

- Andy Woods

  - *https://slbc.org/media/sermon-archives/* (especially the series on Daniel, Revelation, and The Rapture)

- Brannon Howse at WVW (current and historical events from a biblical worldview)

  - *http://www.worldviewweekend.com/*

- Floyd Jones (variety of rich, in-depth Bible teaching)

  - *https://floydnolenjonesministries.com/Audio1.html*

- Blue Letter Bible (free online Bible study tools)

  - *https://www.blueletterbible.org/*

Bibliography

Goldberg, G. J. *Chronology of the War According to Josephus Part 6: The Factions Battle for Power January 68 - May 70 CE*, Accessed January 25, 2024. *www. josephus.org/FlJosephus2/warChronology6Factions. htm.*

Jones, Floyd Nolen. *Chronology of the Old Testament.* Green Forest, AR. New Leaf Publishing Group, 2009.

Woods, Andy. *The Falling Away : A Second Look at 2 Thessalonians 2:3: Spiritual Departure of Physical Rapture?* Taos, NM: Dispensational Publishing House, Inc., 2018.

Woods, Andy. *The Middle East Meltdown: The Islamic Invasion of Israel.* Taos, NM: Dispensational Publishing House, Inc., 2016.

About the Author

Dave Reineke is a dedicated student of Scripture with a particular passion for eschatology, the study of end-times prophecy. "While I read the Bible from time to time when I was young, I wasn't saved until I was 34 (in 2000) and then I earnestly started to study it."

Though not formally trained in seminary, Dave has applied his skills as a university professor to years of meticulous Bible study, compiling his research into a ten-part teaching series that eventually became this book.

He encourages believers to adopt a Berean approach, carefully examining the Scriptures to gain a clearer understanding of God's plan for the culmination of history. Through his work, Dave seeks to bring hope, comfort, and clarity to all who long to explore the depths of biblical prophecy.

Dispensational Publishing House is striving to become the go-to source for Bible-based materials from the dispensational perspective.

Our goal is to provide high-quality doctrinal and worldview resources that make dispensational theology accessible to people at all levels of understanding.

Visit our blog regularly to read informative articles from both known and new writers.

And please let us know how we can better serve you.

Dispensational Publishing House, Inc.
PO Box 3181
Taos, NM 87571

Call us toll free 844-321-4202

www.DispensationalPublishing.com